Foreword by Bis

WEATHERING THE STORM

LEADING IN UNCERTAIN TIMES

DR. DON BRAWLEY III | DR. SAMUEL R. CHAND

iNFLUENCERS
PUBLISHING

Foreword by Bishop Dale C. Bronner

WEATHERING THE STORM

LEADING IN UNCERTAIN TIMES

DR. DON BRAWLEY III | DR. SAMUEL R. CHAND

INFLUENCERS
PUBLISHING

Published by:
Influencers Publishing
PO Box 390820
Snellville, Georgia 30039
770.979.4610

Cover by Influencers Publishers
Text Design by Marlon B. Villadiego

ISBN #978-0-9971692-6-3

Dr. Don Brawley III
Influencers Global
PO Box 390820
Snellville, GA 30039
770-979-4610
www.InfluencersGlobal.com

ENDORSEMENTS

In my book "Church Shift" I talk about the church impacting every aspect of society. This type of radical transformation only occurs intentionally and not by accident. Dr. Brawley & Dr. Chand do a masterful job of showing leaders how to intentionally use change for personal and organizational transformation. I highly recommend every pastor and those who lead beside them read it!

Pastor Sunday Adelaja, Pastor,
Embassy of God, Ukraine

If you have a calling, this book is for you. If you have a vision this book is for you. If you have a future this book is for you. If you are a leader this book is for you. Allow Dr. Brawley and Dr. Chand to walk alongside you as you progress today and plan for tomorrow.

Pastor Dayo Adeyokunu, US Leadership Development Coordinator, Church of the Redeemed

Leadership is hard work in stable times. It is certainly more challenging in uncertain times. You can't control the changes around you but you can position your congregation to benefit from them. I highly recommend *Weathering the Storm: Leading in Uncertain Times* to any church leader that wants to be effective despite uncertainty.

Pastor Mike Buster, Executive Pastor,
Preston Woods Baptist Church, Dallas, Texas

If there was ever a book that was precisely on time, it's *Weathering the Storm: Leading in Uncertain Times.* Here are principles for successful leadership that come from having lived them, not just talked about them... Dr. Brawley and Dr. Chand will encourage, provoke and challenge you to outlast your storms - and they give you the practical tools to do it. Some books are a good read, some a must read, this a book with wisdom critical to your future success.

Paul Louis Cole, President,
Christian Men's Network Worldwide

In *Weathering the Storm: Leading in Uncertain Times* Dr. Brawley and Dr. Chand do a remarkable job at correlating natural disasters to contemporary leadership challenges. They provide the reader with bite-sized solutions for longevity in leadership and ministry. Any leader who desires to stand the test of time needs this book.

Dr. David Cooper, Senior Pastor,
Mount Paran Church of God, Atlanta, Georgia

Never before have we seen so many dynamic changes occur at such an alarming rate. The world we once knew is gone. This presents unique challenges for Christian leaders. *Weathering the Storm: Leading in Uncertain Times* is a great read for leading through the implications of uncertainty.

Dr. Bryan Crute, Senior/Founding Pastor, Destiny Metropolitan Church, Atlanta, Georgia

In the 21st Century local leaders will become global influencers. God will place the world at the finger-tips of his prayerful, prepared, and positioned leaders. Dr. Brawley and Dr. Chand help you take care of home so you can go and reach the world for God.

Reverend Ziga Emmanuel, Pastor,
Grace for All Nations, Seattle, Washington

When I heard Dr. Brawley and Dr. Chand joined forces I knew it would be incredible! Wow! This is a must read for ALL pastors, staff, and volunteers that want to endure these challenging times.

Pastor R. Benjamin Gaither, Senior Pastor, Stronghold Christian Church, Lithonia, Georgia

Dr. Chand and Dr. Brawley are both a leader 's leader. If you want insight, understanding and empowerment to make change your friend, this book is for you. If you want your ministry to sustain another ten years, this book is for you and your leaders.

Dr. Sherry Gaither, Pastor,
Stronghold Christian Church, Lithonia, Georgia

In my book *Marketing your Church for Growth* I consider the implications change has on the church's future outreach strategies. *Weathering the Storm: Leading in Uncertain Times* is a must read for Christian leaders who want to benefit from and influence change happening around them. Doing so may produce the best and most cost effective marketing strategy available today.

Bishop Gary Hawkins, Founding Pastor,
Voices of Faith Ministries, Stone Mountain, Georgia

Our country is experiencing a deficit beyond our struggling economy. Our greatest deficit is a lack of God-honoring leadership. Once that is filled, our other challenges will follow-suite. In *Weathering the Storm: Leading in Uncertain Times,* Dr. Brawley and Dr. Chand offer insightful strategies for pastors and Christian leaders poised to fill that vacuity in the days ahead.

Dr. Benson Karanja, President,
Beulah Heights University, Atlanta, Georgia

As I travel the world, I see one thing leaders have in common; uncertainty. Whether I'm in Africa, America, or Europe I observe leaders searching for direction and answers. Search no longer. This book has the answers you've been looking for!

Apostle Anselm Madubuko, Pastor,
The Revival Assembly, Lagos, Nigeria

We are living in an age of dynamic change where few things are certain. I talk about this in my book, *The Principles and Benefits of Change.* How we interpret and respond to change greatly determines the quality of life we experience. It also influences whether or not we accomplish our divine assignment. Dr. Brawley and Dr. Chand successfully empower leaders to fulfill their assignment by initiating the changes necessary to weather uncertain times.

Dr. Myles Monroe, Founder,
Bahamas Faith Ministries, Nassau, Bahamas

Living on the Gulf of Mexico, I know about storms. During our last hurricane, we survived because we planned for the storm by preparing a "storm kit" filled with fresh water, candles, first aid and food. Dr. Brawley's book is a storm kit that will help you survive the dehydration, darkness, injuries and famine that your storms will bring. Prepare Now!

Bishop John Wade II, D.P.M., Senior Pastor,
The Pentecostal Worship Center/CEO Leadership for Life,
Panama City, Florida

There is an old adage that has historically been used in project planning or preparing for life and death situations. One version of it says, "Prior planning and preparation prevents poor performance". If you want to circumvent poor performance or even an organizational disaster, this is your book!

Rev. Woodrow Walker II, Pastor,
Abundant Life Church, Lithonia, Georgia

TABLE OF CONTENTS

ACKNOWLEDGEMENTS

By Dr. Don Brawley III

Thanks to all the people who have shaped my spirituality, thinking, and personal development over the past three decades. This book is written because of you. To every pastor that works in the trenches and serves on the frontlines, this book is written for you. Finally, for all those who dare to lead, may this work inspire you to outlast your storm. We are in it together.

To the Canaan Land Church International family, I say thank you for your loyal love, committed service, and continual support. Thank you for trusting me to lead you and speak into your lives. Thank you for the honor of allowing me to shepherd you. Your consistent love and committed faith inspires me. Together we will outlast our stormy weather. There is no other church like you; none!

To my executive assistant and sister, Dana Anderson, you know I couldn't do what I do without you. Thanks for serving in excellence and always making me look good! Great is your reward in heaven!

Dawn Mabra, my sister, thanks for your detailed and thorough editing of this manuscript. You did a great job!

A special thanks to all the men and women of God who endorsed my work. You are leaders I truly respect and admire. Thank you for your time and support. Thank you for the blessing you are to me. I am indebted to you.

To my coauthor, Dr. Samuel R. Chand, I am honored that you would write with me. Thanks for your belief in me and continual support. Thanks for the wisdom you impart and the sacrifices you make so others may succeed. Thanks for holding my ladder! May the life you live be the legacy you leave within others, including myself.

To Bishop Dale C. Bronner, wow! Beyond your extreme giftedness, you are a man of great character, nobility, and integrity. All who know you realize you are a gem in God's kingdom. I am richer for having you in my life.

Mona, my wife of over twenty years, I love you dearly. You are my wife, lover, and best friend. You believed in me before I did. You saw my potential and then supported me so I could live it out. You've loved me through stormy weather. I love you with all my heart. By God's grace, we will see another twenty plus years together.

To my favorite three kids in the world, Brandon, Chantelle, and Aaron, daddy loves you. I pray my legacy lives within you and that you surpass everything I ever accomplish. Brandon, my first born, you made it through your tumor storm with great grace, peace, and faith. You are intelligent and anointed. That's a great combination! Chantelle, my only daughter and princess, you are beautiful, intelligent, and can do whatever you put your mind to do; for real. Thanks for helping me with the cover of this book. Aaron you are multitalented, smart, and keep me young! Soon you'll be able to illustrate my book covers. I love your heart for God's people.

To my brother, Rev. David K. Brawley, thanks for having my back! To all my other family and friends, you know I love you and thank God we are connected.

Finally and above all, I thank God for Jesus Christ my savior, friend, and travel guide through uncertain times. When others left, you never turned away. I live to hear you say two words, "well done." It is this hope that makes everything else worthwhile.

DEDICATION

I lovingly dedicate this book to my parents, Don Brawley, Jr. and Desiree Brawley. I am who I am because of you. Dad, thanks for pushing me to aim higher when I was satisfied with getting B's in elementary school! Thanks for putting a champion spirit within me. Mom, look at the fruit of your labor. All of this is a result of you weathering your storm. It's because you made it, that I made it. Thanks for putting your kids before yourself. I love you both dearly.

FOREWORD

The notion that we are living and leading in the same world we led in yesterday is an erroneous belief. Yesterday, for the most part, pastors and other leaders only needed to concern themselves with the changes in their own communities. This is no longer true. Holding on to this type of antiquated thinking hinders leaders from profiting from opportunities change brings and preparing for its insidious dangers.

Today we live in a high-tech, fast-paced, and interconnected world. No longer are our neighbors limited to those who live in the same geographic area as we live but those who share the same greater global community during our lifetimes. Changing dynamics in their world often influences change in ours. Conversely, the same is true. Let me give you an example.

Although I live in metropolitan Atlanta, when Hurricane Katrina struck the Gulf Coast it affected me. Hundreds of thousands of Katrina evacuees flooded into the greater Atlanta area. It impacted our city in multiply ways including its workforce, traffic, economy, and social dynamics to name a few. However, it didn't stop there.

It also directly impacted our membership. In an instant gas prices skyrocketed and gas stations even ran out of fuel. Overtime people became choosy about how far they would travel to attend church. While some of those who lived further away from our campus decided not to travel as far we were able to optimize our outreach efforts during this time. You see, we narrowed our focus on those within a five mile radius of our ministry. As a result, we didn't experience the loss of attendance or revenue that other churches encountered.

Not only are churches affected by disasters but so are businesses. The collapse of the US housing market and the instability of Wall Street have either directly or indirectly caused businesses great loss. Many established companies permanently closed their doors.

All it takes is one disaster to forever close your ministry. A few bad storms, a fast spreading pandemic disease, or a failing economy can swiftly become the proverbial straw that breaks the camel's back. Unfortunately many churches, like so many Americans, live "week to week." Are you prepared? Are your leaders prepared to lead others as change becomes the new norm?

This is what *Weathering the Storm: Leading in Uncertain Times* is all about. It's about leadership. It's about foresight. It's about outlasting your storm.

Please don't misunderstand me. *Weathering the Storm: Leading in Uncertain Times* isn't a book about natural disasters. Actually, very little in this book even addresses natural disasters. Instead it is an insightful guide about preparation, leadership, and change. This book shows you how to fortify your organization despite change.

You may be going through changes right now. Perhaps you are fighting against competing agendas? Maybe conflict is burning throughout your church? It could be a rift in your leadership team. It might be that you are carrying pain from a recent church hurt or even a split. I don't know what storm you are weathering. I do know despite your storm, right now in your hand, you hold a key to your enduring success.

As a pastor or leader in the local church you will forever face change and the uncertainty it brings. Don't go at it alone. Regardless if the storm you face is within your church or without, I recommend you make this book your travel companion. I know Dr. Brawley and Dr. Chand quite well. Both men are leaders. Both men are servants. Both are change strategists. Allow their wisdom, wit, and wealth of experience to walk with you as you weather your storm and lead others through theirs.

Bishop Dale C. Bronner, D. Min.
Author/Senior Pastor
Word of Faith Family Worship Cathedral
Atlanta, GA

INTRODUCTION

The watershed difference between those who grow stronger and those who barely survive in meeting the challenges of change are these four committed beliefs:

- "Life is difficult."

- "If you would only accept how tough life is, you would find it much, much easier." (advice offered by the financier J.P. Morgan to his son)

- "What doesn't kill you ONLY makes you stronger IF you learn from it."

- "We can't wait for the storm [of change] to pass. We'll all have to learn to work in the rain." (P. Silas, Chairman of Phillips Petroleum)

Many years ago, while in college, I (Dr. Brawley) worked as a telephone customer service representative for a national eyewear company. There I met a young lady named Liz. Whenever incoming calls slowed down Liz would pause and tell me new stories from her latest escapades.

Liz was a hilarious young lady. During our few years at the same company I listened regularly as she told her adventurous tales. Over the course of time, she met her husband, married, and began her "bargain" travels. We always laughed and agreed that the drama she'd experienced could only happen to her.

Liz always looked for travel steals I mean deals. To date, she's still the only person I know that could plan a weekend trip, for two, from Long Island to Virginia for under a hundred dollars! Not only that, but she'd tell how she'd spent less than she originally planned! There was one bargain trip though she'd wished she'd never taken.

One weekend, Liz and her husband went off on another "economic" escapade. Unfortunately, they both got more than they bargained for. They flew from Long Island's Mac Arthur airport with Albany New York as their destination. Anyone who knows just a little about New York City area airports knows Mac Arthur airport is small, very small, okay tiny. Often, particularly in the eighties, that meant traveling on a small commuter sized plane. This was the beginning of drama.

When Liz saw the size of the plane she all but refused to get on it. She said it had less than ten rows and she was scared for her life. However, with a little coaching from her husband she boarded the plane and the two of them were off to Albany.

Suddenly, in mid-flight, the plane experienced horrific turbulence. The turbulence was the result of a storm. Liz cried out and went into an awful frenzy. In her fearful state she screamed at the flight attendant, "What's going on? Are we going to make it?" The flight attendant turned around and all Liz could see were tears running down her cheeks as she screamed back, "I don't know!" Needless to say that didn't help Liz at all. If I recall correctly, Liz quickly spiraled downhill from being in a frenzy to having a panic attack right about then!

Unlike Liz's flight to Albany, our turbulence is not temporary nor the uncertainty that accompanies it. Globalization, technological advances, the World Wide Web, and rapid transportation have already solidified its permanent position. Continual change is both permanent and eminent. It is the new order of the day and it will continue to be so. In fact, in the days ahead, change will occur faster and more frequently while impacting a greater number of people.

Change is not inherently good or bad. It is how we handle change that determines if it works against us or in our favor. For the ill prepared, change can completely wipe them out. However, for those that anticipate and position themselves accordingly, it opens up a new world of possibilities and subsequently opportunities!

> *Opportunities of a lifetime must be seized in the lifetime of the opportunity.*
> ~ Linda Bravenport

Leaders must decide if they will benefit or break from change and the feelings of uncertainty that accompany it. You see, when it comes to the pressure that change and uncertainty produces you are either a pipe or a diamond. One breaks under pressure, the other is made under it. This has tremendous repercussions for 21st century leaders, those who walk alongside them, and ultimately their organizations.

For a moment, let's go back to Liz and her horrific flight. Let's say you were the pilot flying the plane that day. Essentially, you were the senior organizational leader. As such, you recognize each life onboard is ultimately under your stewardship and responsibility. So what would you do if you knew you were flying through a storm?

I'm not a pilot, but I assume you'd do *everything possible* to ensure you safely and successfully navigated the storm and arrived at your intended destination. Moreover, I believe you would want a co-pilot and crew with both the heart and ability to do the same.

Perhaps the worst thing that you could do as a pilot in a storm is flying as if there weren't one. Imagine how dangerous it would be if a pilot never told his passengers to remain seated with their seatbelt fastened. What if he ignored critical warnings and other essential information on his monitor? How about if he never adjusted his flying altitude or *constantly* corrected his course through the storm? What if he just flew without a specific flight plan?

Problem 1: Unlike a licensed pilot, most leaders haven't been trained on how to lead through uncertain times.

If you are a pastor or any other organizational leader, you are the pilot we are writing to. We want you to arrive at your set destination even if it means you have to re-navigate your route. We want you to be successful despite the uncertainty that accompanies turbulent change. We also know your success is heavily dependent on those that serve with you.

Furthermore, as the pilot I assume you'd want all your crew members on the same page as you. This means they would have clarity concerning your mission and the capacity to effectively weather any adverse conditions that may arise on your journey. After all, you can't get to your destination without your crew.

Moreover, your crew determines if your passengers have a pleasant or unpleasant experience since they directly interface with them. Your crew is your leaders. How your leaders handle turbulent storms, continual change and uncertain times directly affects your people.

The flight attendant that served my friend did more damage than good. In the absence of seeing the pilot's face and hearing his voice the passengers looked to her for direction and hope. Instead they found confusion and fear. Consequently, in one day that airline permanently lost at least two customers. As you've seen the flight attendant did not give the direction and hope her passengers sought. My guess is she didn't give it because she didn't have it.

Problem 2: Like the flight attendant above, non-senior leaders often struggle with holding their crew together in uncertain times.

The same is true for leaders. They can't give what they don't have. In times of turbulence, crises, and change people look to them more than they do during stable and predictable times. In fact, it could be argued that people don't really need leaders during stable times; they only need coordinators of processes, people, and events. However, during times of instability, uncertainty, and change leaders are not only needed, they are desperately sought after. Friend, as you will see, that time is now.

The only thing on earth that remains the same is change. Think about that for a moment. Everything changes over time. Styles change. Communities change. Economies change. Our bodies change. Even land formations change over time. Obviously, this is not new. However, what is new is how change occurs and will continue occurring.

We predict fast-paced, high impact, and continual change is here to stay. As a result, people will look to you and your leaders more than ever before for direction and a sense of security. For that reason, as a leader anywhere in an organization you need to prepare and equip yourself and those flying with you for leading in uncertain and turbulent times. This is what this book is all about.

> **Problem 3:** Change makes leaders more in demand and leading more demanding!

We have written this book for Christian leaders of ministries, departments, businesses, and entire organizations. We intend for it to be a catalyst of conversation as you wrestle with the ideas and principles found herein and how they fit your context. We will not give you all the answers, but hopefully we will inspire you to ask new questions, lead with greater intentionality, unify your organization, and develop the resiliency and adaptability needed to weather any storm.

Problem 4: Storms can lead to disasters.

What is a storm? We've all been through one before. A storm is a violent disturbance of the atmosphere. Often this disturbance is accompanied with physical manifestations we call strong winds, rain, thunder, lightning, and snow. At one time or another, each of us has encountered a violent disturbance within the atmosphere we live.

We've all faced storms that have directly affected our family, church, community, organization or business. In some cases we've lived through multiply storms simultaneously in each category! While I said that with a bit of jest it is actually something to celebrate. The fact that we've come through the storm and are still here to bear witness is enough cause for rejoicing.

Unfortunately, not everybody survives stormy weather. If you pause and reflect for a moment I'm sure you can easily think of a person who didn't survive their last storm. Some marriages did not survive their last storm. There are churches that didn't survive their last storm. Some airlines, franchises, banks, and Fortune 500 companies did not survive their last storm. As we write there are entire industries in jeopardy of being completely shut down because of violent disturbances in the atmosphere. Yet there are others that have been hit by a storm and yet seem to weather it better than their counterparts.

How is it that one company can go through a storm and when the storm is through they are too? Meanwhile another company encounters similar conditions, yet successfully rides it out. How is it that during a recession some churches report a decrease in giving, up to thirty percent, while others in the same city report an increase in giving? As strange as it is our church (Dr. Brawley) is having its strongest financial year in fifteen years, in the middle of an economic downturn. Finally, how is it that several companies in the World Trade Center faced the same disaster on the same day, yet some never reopened while others did only a few days thereafter?

What makes the difference? There are many factors; however, I can tell you two factors probably make the biggest difference. They are leadership and preparation. The changes and challenges storms bring require innovative, insightful, and courageous leaders capable of leading through their fierceness. Often, these leaders are unaware of their own leadership ability until it manifests in the midst of dire circumstances we call storms. Unfortunately, storms often give way to disasters.

As the winds of change have increased so has the likelihood of a disaster occurring. A disaster is anything that significantly affects your ability to carry out the critical functions necessary for your organizational mission and ongoing operation. While a catastrophic event such as an earthquake could cause a disaster, a non-catastrophic event that causes significant impact on your church or company's ability to perform and its longterm viability is also a disaster. Here are just some possible disasters:

- The quick spread of a pandemic disease i.e. the Swine Flu, Bird Flu or the Dog Flu. (Hey, you never know). People abstain from public meetings thus causing a significant decrease in the revenue you receive from your donors or customers.

- Seemingly forgotten information reappears, through powerful search mechanisms on-line, and renders a senior or top leader non-credible overnight.

- Significant decrease in human resources.

- A fire destroys all or part of your facility.

- Moral failure within your leadership team.

- Cyber attack or loss of critical data.

- Death of a senior leader.

- Sustained power or utility outage.

- Your computer crashes and important files are not backed up.

- Hurricane, tornado, & other natural storms.

- Terrorist acts or threats impede your organization's work.

- Gas prices skyrocket overnight and limit how far people are willing to drive for your services.

In this book, we will discuss the organizational equivalent of some of these disasters. We will also consider how you can possibly prevent some, prepare for others, and recover from them all. Finally, we will give you the blue prints you need to prepare for any actual physical disasters. If you follow through on these recommendations you will significantly increase the probability that your doors remain open despite stormy weather and unforeseen changes happening around you.

BEFORE WE START

We've teamed up and written this book for several reasons:

- First, we both have a heart for God's church and the local pastors that lead them. Both of us have pastoral experience and understand the tremendous burden carried by those who lead.

- Secondly, we are all in it together. If you fail, we fail. If we fail you fail. Not only do we want you to survive the storms of change but thrive in the midst of them. Doing so brings God glory on earth and carries eternal ramifications. For us and for you, failure is not an option!

- Finally, we both consult pastors, senior leaders
  and visionaries through their personal uncertainty
  and organizational challenges towards visionary
  outcomes. We want to share our experiences,
  mistakes, perspectives, and insights.

This book is formatted accordingly. There are seven chapters, six of which have two parts and the last containing teaching points and discussion questions. Dr. Brawley starts the chapter by introducing its concepts and offers the reader an expanded and in-depth consideration of the subject matter. Dr. Chand follows-up and concludes the chapter with ingenious and witty illustrations, examples, and exhortations. Each writer's vantage point compliments the other and taken together provide the reader with well rounded and thought provoking content with immediate take away value.

May God bless and increase you in ways that your mind cannot completely conceive of now. May you be better for the storms that have come your way. Finally, may God grant you and your tribe the resources to weather any storm and lead in these uncertain times.

Dr. Don Brawley III
Influencers Global
www.InfluencersGlobal.com

Dr. Samuel R. Chand
Samuel R. Chand Consulting
www.SamChand.com

1

WEATHERING THE STORM:
Leading in Uncertain Times

Dr. Don Brawley III

PLANNING—WHAT'S THE BIG IDEA?

If you don't know where you are going,

you will probably end up somewhere else.

~ Laurence Johnson Peter

My wife and I love to travel. We've traveled all over the country and even across the world for the past twenty plus years. Traveling has been very adventurous and invigorating for us. We've sailed into the Atlantic Ocean, snorkeled in the Caribbean Sea, rode horseback through wooded trails, climbed high heights on rock walls, swam with dolphins, zip-lined through exotic places and paras- ailed over deep blue ocean waters.

One thing we can say about traveling is that it requires planning. Although planning doesn't guarantee your travels will go smoothly, it certainly increases the odds! Before we plan any trip we take time to envision our destination.

> **Unfortunately, too many leaders have borrowed their vision from others and internalized it as their own.**

We start with a vision. Will we recline on a beach in the Bahamas or tour London or Italy? Is this trip for sightseeing or re- laxation? Our vision tells us the direction we will take and lets us know when we've arrived. This holds true for leaders and those who journey with them. This reminds me of an unforgettable story.

We have a friend whose mother booked a flight from New York to Palm Springs, California. She was on her way to a conference and could hardly wait to get there. She boarded her plane in New York and off she was to her destination. At least that's what she thought.

A few hours later, she landed and de-boarded the plane. She quickly retrieved her bags and hailed a taxi. She gave her driver the name of the hotel that held her reservations and off they went. Then something went wrong. Okay, something went severely wrong.

The taxi driver could not find the hotel that my friend's mother reserved. The one he took her to, although the same franchise name wasn't the address she gave him. "Sir, this is not my hotel." she said. He argued, "This is the only hotel with that name in the city."

After circling around town for nearly an hour, both the driver and my friend's mother were annoyed with each other. In her frustration, my friend's mother read aloud the *complete* address of her hotel one more time. Instantly, it became clear to the driver why there was so much confusion. "You're not in Palm Springs, California. You're in Palm Springs, Florida." he exclaimed! Needless to say, this *minor* error cost her extra money and time.

It took years before I could fully understand how she ended up in Florida instead of California. I guess I could see how a person could board the wrong plane if they were not paying attention to the signs. Perhaps, she was asleep when the pilot told his passengers the local temperature in Florida! But how do you explain driving around Florida (which is extremely flat) and thinking you're in California (which is extremely mountainous)?

Years later the answer is crystal clear to me. My friend's mother did not have a vision for where she was headed. She didn't have a clear picture of her destination. Although she made plans, she didn't have a vision. Vision, clear vision, always proceeds planning.

Pilots depart with a vision for where they will land. They have clarity regarding the locale of their next stop. Although stormy weather may come and they may have to deviate from their original flight plan, they always know the general direction they are headed and the specifics of their final destination.

That's the power of vision. Vision keeps you headed in the right direction despite unforeseen obstacles. It helps you creatively navigate through challenges. Vision motivates you to keep moving until what you've envisioned becomes a tangible reality.

Unfortunately, too many leaders have borrowed their vision from others and internalized it as their own. This only causes unnecessary frustration, stress, cost, and even confusion. This is not unlike landing in Palm Springs, Florida instead of Palm Springs, California.

Knowing your specific destination prior to moving forward is essential. How else would you know if you were truly successful when you arrived there? Not knowing could bring devastation; particularly if you ended up in the wrong place. It would be like climbing the ladder of success and reaching the top only to discover your ladder was leaning against the wrong building! That's why you can't measure your success by someone else's ladder or vision. Only your vision tells you what success looks like for you and those traveling alongside you.

> **Not knowing could be like climbing the ladder of success and reaching the top only to discover your ladder was leaning against the wrong building!**

So what is vision anyway? Vision is simply your preferred future state. It's where you're supposed to arrive after some time.

Just like my friend's mother, you have a specific destination that you're supposed to arrive at. While many people planned to leave New York and arrive in Florida that day, she was supposed to be in California. Arriving at someone else's destination is always at best disappointing.

Most Christian leaders would never argue about the need for a vision; however, planning is often times thought of as *unspiritual.* However, nothing could be farther from the truth.

Scripture shows God Himself is a planner. Creation was planned. Redemption was planned too. Even eternity is planned. God is a planner and every leader needs to plan too. In fact a plan is probably more essential when leading in uncertain and changing times.

THREE THINGS YOU NEED TO LEAD IN UNCERTAIN TIMES

1. A clear VISION of your destination.

    *   What will it look like when you arrive there? Describe it with as much detail as possible. It has been said that nothing is dynamic until it is specific.

    *   How will you know when you have arrived at your destination? What will you see? Who will we see? What will they be doing?

    `• Note: a building is never the vision. Vision always encompasses the lives that will be changed by your mission and purpose. Buildings are only tools. They are mere means to an end not the ends themselves.

2. A flight plan (STRATEGY)—this is your specific plan for getting to your *preferred future* (vision) also called your destination. As I consult pastors across the US, I am amazed by how many leaders have adopted *other people's strategies* (OPS) as their own. While your strategy may **Think of strategy as your unique formula for success.** resemble another's it should be individualized to fit your unique context. Otherwise you too will wind up in Palm Springs, Florida instead of Palm Springs, California! Think of strategy as your unique formula for success.

3. Disaster recovery plan (CONTINGENCY PLAN)—you will never leave a US airport without hearing something like, "In the event of an emergency or if cabin pressure

suddenly drops..." The odds are more likely that you'll have an accident on the way to or from the airport than on a plane. Yet, a *disaster recovery plan* (DPR) is both mandated and in place for you. Unfortunately, things don't always go according to plan. For this reason you need a DPR. Here are a few questions to get you thinking:

- What in our flight/strategic plan could go wrong?

- How can we prevent future challenges by preparing today?

- What delays could occur and how will we handle them?

- Is the cost of doing nothing (to prepare for a disaster) worth jeopardizing our mission? Asked another way, is our vision valuable enough to defend it through preparation?

DISASTER PREVENTION AND RECOVERY PLANNING

The bad news: disasters are inevitable.

The good news: preparation *significantly* increases your probability of survival!

Before we go any further, I need to settle something. Preparing for a disaster does not mean you don't have faith. Nor does it mean you are not spiritual. If anything, it shows you are a faithful steward over what God has entrusted to you. In fact it is foolish not to plan for something that is inevitable.

Moreover, none of us can presume we fully know God's will, all that he has planned, or the totality of what is to come. Neither can we be so naive to think that just because we are believers the affects of disasters won't touch us or our organizations. Consider Jesus' parable about building your house on a rock rather than sand.

In this parable Jesus doesn't say to build just in case a storm comes, but for "when" the storm comes and "when" the winds blow. His parable also shows how preparing for a disaster leads to surviving it. Despite his teachings many Christians believe they are *exempt* from trouble not to mention disasters. I understand this faulty belief system because long ago I used to think this way too. This is why they don't prepare for them.

Let me say, I'm not so much advocating for disasters as I am planning for your recovery. Even if God exempted all believers and religious organizations from disaster we would have to still deal with their *indirect* affects. If a disaster affects:

- Your neighborhood businesses or community schools, it ultimately affects you.

- Our nation's economy, it ultimately affects you.

- The airline or auto industry, it impacts how you travel.

- Our nations housing market, it impacts your home's value.

- The major stock markets in Europe or Asia, it impacts the stock market your retirement is connected to.

In retrospect we've seen how our churches, organizations, and families exist within a greater system and just how intricately connected we are as a global community. What happens on one side of the world quickly and almost without obstruction impacts the other side of the world. AT&T's motto, "We're all connected" has never been truer than it is today.

GOD—A DISASTER RECOVERY PLANNER?

I can hear someone thinking, "Okay where is he going with this?" Just stick with me for one moment. You'll soon see how

God prepared for a disaster before it ever occurred. In fact, He was the first person to design a recovery plan!

Let's go back to the beginning, the book of Genesis. You know the account. God made everything man would need and by the sixth day created him in His own image. Things were going just great until Adam sinned.

Adam's sin led to the greatest disaster ever experienced on planet earth. In fact, Adam's sin is the root cause of every other disaster we experience today. It set the process of both spiritual and physical death into motion. His sin led to:

- Sickness & disease
- Broken families and relationships
- Envy, strife, and murder
- Humanism
- Idolatry
- Rivaling agendas
- Inferior governmental systems
- And many more consequences—too many to list.

None of the above seems to depict God's original plan for His new creation or world.

GOD PLANNED FOR A FAMILY

God's original plan was to have and enjoy a family. To this end God specifically planned. Just like an expecting couple prepares for the arrival of their firstborn God put everything his children would need in place before their arrival.

First, He made the heavens and the earth so His family would have a suitable home. Second, He created grass and seed- bearing fruit for food. Third, He hung the sun and moon in space so His family would have light. God followed these acts by creating birds, fish, and every kind of animal. Finally, He made male and

I call it a disaster recovery plan; however, you might be more familiar with its Biblical terminology, "redemption"!

female in his image and they bore his family resemblance.

Unfortunately, sin soon marred that resemblance. Once Adam sinned he brought death into God's new creation. Till this day, sin's devastating effects still keep all of creation groaning and travailing for the total recovery of God's original design.

Certainly, this was far from what God planned when he created his new world and family. Yet this became his reality and is not unlike what we experience when a disaster occurs. We start a business, ministry or even a family with a vision. Next we develop a plan for realizing that vision. Before we know it, we start realizing our vision. Then...then...no way... then...no please God no...Oh yes, then comes a disaster!

NOW WHAT?

Clearly, things did not go as God planned or did they? I think it is safe to say God did not want Adam to make the choice he made. However, despite Adam's choice and its resulting disaster, God had a plan! He had a disaster recovery plan and as a leader you need one too.

In Genesis chapter three God foretells of Jesus' triumphant defeat over sin and satan. He says, "You shall bruise his heel and the seed of the woman shall crush his head". The rest of the Bible, in one way or another, details God's disaster recovery plan and its fulfillment. I call it a disaster recovery plan; however, you might be more familiar with its Biblical terminology, "redemption"!

Redemption can mean the act of saving someone or something. It also denotes paying a price for something to regain possession of it. Essentially, you need a plan of redemption for your organization, ministry, and family that ensures it survives a disaster and that afterwards you can reclaim it for its intended purpose.

> **...you significantly increase your odds of total recovery when you plan for it.**

As you know redemption costs something. It cost God His only begotten Son and it cost His Son His life. Disaster recovery will cost you too. It will cost you on two sides of the same continuum.

It will cost you on the front side. By front side I am referring to *before* a disaster occurs. Prior to a disaster the biggest price you pay is time. You only need a DRP if you truly love and value what God's given you. If it is of little value to you, don't waste your time. However, if you truly value your organization, your family, the people God has given you and your collective destiny you must plan like it. You need planning time to consider all your future options *prior* to an array of plausible disasters and adequate thought time to completely work through them. Additionally, you'll need time to determine all your critical functions and inventory the tools necessary for ongoing operations. (I'll explain this later).

The alternative side of the continuum in DRP is *after* a disaster strikes. The actual cost you pay on the back end is unknown now. However, one thing has proven true. The cost of recovery is far less on the back end when you pay the price of time on the front end. In fact, you significantly increase your odds of total recovery when you plan for it. There are other benefits you'll experience if you plan before a disaster comes:

- Less stress—you won't have to make a plan. Instead, you work your plan and let your plan work for you.

- Reduced uncertainty—since disasters all bring a degree of uncertainty having a plan in place tells you and your flight crew what your next step should be.

- Collaborative effort—all stake-holders will be on the same page during the disaster because they helped create the plan.

- Less financial burden—the longer it takes to get back to normal operations the more it will cost you.

- Faster and more successful recovery.

We've determined that having a DRP is scriptural, cost effective, and demonstrates good stewardship. Additionally, we have seen how our all-sufficient and omniscient God, who knows the future, modeled DRP. Finally, we see how DRP can ultimately keep your doors open, save your mission, protect your vision, and limit your losses. Now that you know there's only one question—what are you waiting for?

Come on. Let's get started. One day you'll be glad you did!

1

WEATHERING THE STORM:
Leading in Uncertain Times

Dr. Samuel R. Chand

Visionary Strategic Planning (VSP) has three components:

- Visionary

- Strategic

- Planning

VISIONARY assumes there is a vision. In layman's terms vision is where you're going. Only those with vision plan. If my vision was to travel from Atlanta where I reside to Los Angeles to speak at a conference or consult with an organization then it will necessitate some planning. Let's look at some of those components for planning:

Only those with vision plan.

- I receive the invitation and then have to ascertain if the organization inviting me is congruent with my vision. Everything I do is about leadership, but if the organization is not requesting some type of leadership development then I have to say no.

- On reception of the invitation, my office checks my calendar for availability on the dates requested.

- The flight has to be decided, the ticket purchased and itinerary communicated.

- I have to pack according to the weather, length of my trip, the occasion and my assignment.

…all this even before I leave my house!

Organizational consultants have made "vision" into something esoteric and illusive—it is not. It is knowing where you are going. Leaders KNOW (understand the vision), GROW (embody the vision) and SHOW (lead the vision).

STRATEGIC assumes there is order and not chaos. Strategic implies high levels of intentionality, forethought and perspective. If you are flying from one city to the other it is strategic that you have a boarding pass and government issued identification to pass throughsecurity. It is strategic that you show up in time to catch the flight. It is strategic that you go to the right airlines and terminal. It is strategic that you go to the right gate.

Lack of planning usually is an indicator of lack of significance attached to the event.

PLANNING assumes something is going on or there would be no need to plan. It also assumes that whatever is going on has some degree of significance. Lack of planning usually is an indicator of lack of significance attached to the event.

There are degrees of planning. For example, if you were invited to the White House for dinner your planning will be escalated. In contrast to that if you and some friends were getting together for dinner it would take lesser amount of planning. Don't let the younger generation fool you—their "whatever" is also planned.

Their ultra-casual attire ("I just threw some clothes on.") is planned.

We plan for what we consider important. In my book, *Who Moved Your Ladder?* I use the acronym of DOCTOR to assist some of this planning.

D = Directional (Vision)

O = Objectives (Outcomes)

C = Cash (Resources)

T = Tracking (Accountability)

O = Overall Evaluation (Assessment)

R = Refinements (Adjustments)

Visionary Strategic Planning needs a DOCTOR.

2

FIREFIGHTERS:
Positioned To Protect

Dr. Don Brawley III

Remember the hours after September 11th when
we came together as one to answer the attack against our homeland
We drew strength when our firefighters ran up stairs and risked
their lives so that others might live; when rescuers rushed into
smoke and fire at the Pentagon; when the men and women of Flight
93 sacrificed themselves to save our nation's Capitol; when flags
were hanging from front porches all across America, and strangers
became friends. It was the worst day we have ever seen,
but it brought out the best in all of us.

~ Senator John Kerry

Do you remember the 1970's hit television show *All in the Family?* I do. Okay, I'm dating myself here. Anyway, I can still remember the obnoxiously overbearing bigoted main character Archie Bunker, played by Carol O'Conner. Although, O'Conner was only acting as Archie, the role he played was not too far from his own family's background and beliefs. I know because, during my mother 's childhood,

O'Conner 's grandmother and two aunts lived next door to my mother in Jamaica, Queens on 119th Street. Often O'Conner would stay with his family. During this time, he studied acting although my family didn't know it then. For years, his grandmother and aunts would not speak to my grandparents or their children because they were colored. However, one day something happened that forever changed this.

One autumn afternoon, O'Conner 's grandmother was in her backyard raking leaves. She made a pile and then proceeded to burn them. She lit a match and the dry leaves caught on fire. For many people back then, and even today in some places, that was the way to get rid of unwanted leaves. It wasn't setting the leaves on fire that was such a significant event. It was the fact that her housecoat caught on fire with them! Yes, both the pile she raked and the robe she wore went up in smoke that day. The good news is she didn't lose her life, but seemingly she lost her bigotry.

Firefighters are protectors of vision and purpose.

You see, my grandfather worked the night shift and was home sleeping. He heard O'Conner 's grandmother scream. Without thinking twice, Grandpa Francis rushed outside, jumped over the fence that separated the two properties, and threw her to the ground. Ms. O'Conner continued screaming while grandpa rolled her around on the ground and suffocated out the fire that could have severely burned or even killed her.

My mother tells me from that day on the Francis family was always welcomed in the O'Conner family's house. In fact, not a long time thereafter the O'Conner family had a special request for my mother's family. Apparently their television stopped working. They asked if they could watch the *first* episode of Carol O'Conner's new show *All in the Family* at my family's house.

Somehow the "color " barrier no longer existed. It seems as though Ms. O'Conner's leaves and housecoat were not the only thing burned up in the fire that day. Color no longer mattered. In their eyes, grandpa was a hero.

WHO ARE YOUR FIREFIGHTERS?

Unfortunately, pastors spend far too much time fighting fires within their churches. In most churches if a fire doesn't break out in the music department it's because one already started within the deacon's ministry or church staff. Senior leaders are often distracted and hindered by fires. When this happens they are no longer operating at their best within their role. Even worst, their chances of burnout (no pun intended) is significantly increased. Every senior leader needs firefighters, people positioned to protect their vision.

Firefighters are protectors of vision and purpose. Just like your local firemen, there are some things these leaders do regularly to reduce the possibility of conflicting flames breaking out. There are many, but here are a few:

- They *steadily* model behaviors consistent with the organization's shared values

- They *intentionally* establish and *consistently* uphold the unique traditions and rituals that remind people of *who* the organization is

- They *regularly* remind others why they *always* do certain things and *never* do others

- They *silently* teach people how to behave in ways that are consistent with what their organization represents.

However, there is no amount of fire prevention that guarantees a fire will never happen. Unfortunately, there *will* still be fires. They are apart of life. There are two reasons why we need firefighters. The first reason is to prevent them as much as possible. The second reason you need firefighters is to minimize the devastation fires cause.

Anyone who has ever witnessed even the smallest of fires knows the fear a little fire generates in the heart of the unsuspecting victim. Like recent fires that destroyed millions of dollars of property in California and hundreds of miles of acreage in Florida, they often start small, but boy do they spread quickly! Yet, it's not the size of a small fire that generates fear. Rather, it is the potential the fire possesses of quickly spreading and destroying everything in its path that makes your heart pound and the adrenaline rush through your body. Often, it is what you do in the first few moments after a fire begins that determines just how extensive the damage will be.

> **Often, it is what you do in the first few moments after a fire begins that determines just how extensive the damage will be.**

FIRST RESPONDERS

It is the same wherever there is a group of people. It does not matter if it is a family, small business, large company, church, or community organization. There are some people you don't want acting as first responders. I'm sure someone has already popped into your mind after reading this statement. This is because they only pour gas on the flame and make matters worst! You know them. By the time a small issue passes their desk, travels through their phone line, or receives their "two cents" it blows up into an explosion that shakes the entire organization.

This is why it is important that you have firefighters, throughout your organization, positioned to protect your vision. Just like your local firemen, often these firefighters won't just emerge out of the blue. They must be called. So let me make an announcement. There are people called to protect your vision;

however, you must first identify them.

Firefighters are both proactive and reactive. For instance, our local fire department comes by at least once a year to ensure our church building is up to code and that its fire system works correctly. They do their best to ensure the probability of a fire breaking out is minimized. However, if a fire does break out they are in position to protect our people and purpose. They are fast to respond to a fire and do their best to put it out quickly.

Firefighters are first responders and combatants of conflict who:

> **There are people called to protect your vision; however, you must first identify them.**

- *Willingly* take the heat themselves and thereby personally protect your vision.

- *Unreservedly* sacrifice themselves, in the face of trouble, for a cause greater than themselves.

- *Instinctively* and appropriately use the right tools to navigate others out of the danger zone.

- *Quickly* contain the flames of conflict so they don't spread any further.

Once you have identified your first respondents you must equip them with the right tools to get the job done. A firefighter without tools is basically useless. Here are a few basic tool analogies for your consideration. Every firefighter needs:

IDENTIFY THEM:

- A fire-resistant uniform—this represents the heart and mind of your first respondent. If the person is carrying an offense in their heart they will be easily consumed by someone else's fire. First respondents must not be easily sucked into other people's flames.

EQUIP THEM:

- A fire truck—first respondents need the ability and liberty to remain mobile. In other words, they need the authority to drop everything else in the firehouse to extinguish a fire. Also they need an array of accessible tools to fight a fire. Each fire has its own unique set of circumstances and no fire is fought exactly the same way as the one before. Training in conflict management would be useful here.

ENCOURAGE THEM:

- A partner—no one should fight a fire alone. They are too dangerous. Everyone needs support and someone to look out for him or her when they enter the danger zone. Even scripture teaches us to go "two by two". Partners encourage, pray for, and support each other through not so pleasant times.

EMPOWER THEM:

- A ladder—the ladder represents the ability to go as high as necessary to extinguish the fire. In other words, first responders must be empowered with decision-making authority. If a fire breaks out, they don't have time to go through fifty people to get answers, authority, or approval. They need delegated authority to deal with the fire right away. Moreover, they need to know who else up the ladder they can reach if they need additional support.

- A fire hose—a source of power and strength beyond their capacity to extinguish the worst of fires. First respondents need to be full of the Holy Spirit, live under His control, and have a fervent prayer life.

Although this is last on the list, it is undoubtedly the most important. Don't consider anyone who does not meet these criteria. To do so, would be like sending a fireman to put out a fire without any water.

Not the glittering weapon fights the fight,
but rather the hero's heart.

~ Proverb

Who are your firefighters? Identify them. Equip them. Encourage them. Empower them.

Safety doesn't happen by accident.

~ Author Unknown

FIRE RESISTANT

While no article of clothing can be 100% fireproof, like baby clothing, it can be fire resistant if it is made of the right stuff. When something is fire resistant it is for the protection of the person not the clothing. Who cares if your suit is destroyed if your life is preserved?

Often God allows fires in our lives and even in His church to burn away the leaves, those things that are dead, out of season, no longer necessary or he can't use. Perhaps you are facing a fire right now. Don't be dismayed. God may be separating the worthless from the priceless.

> *And if you extract the precious from the worthless,*
>
> *You will become My spokesman…*
>
> ~ Jeremiah 15:19 (NAS)

More often than not, fires are caused by those living in the house rather than someone outside the house. The same is true in organizations. Nearly all fires you'll face will start from people who are *inside* your house.

Fires are one of the most common disasters to disrupt normal operations and completely destroy a house. They are so common and their effects so devastating that we have fire insurance for our homes, businesses, churches, and organizations. Similarly, fires occur more often in our churches than we realize and disrupt us from effective service.

Nearly all fires you'll face will start from people who are *inside* your house.

Organizational fires come in a range of expressions and intensities. For instance in a church a fire could look like:

- Someone leaves the church because of discord and it spreads until others follow behind.

- Two leaders openly disagree and the people who serve with them divide behind them into competing camps.

- A member is jealous because another person was selected for a particular role so she sabotages the other's success.

- Instead of collaborating ministries constantly compete with each other.

I could go on with many other examples. One thing I know for sure is, just like the O'Conner fire, organizational fires always involve people and how leaders respond to fires always determines the damage done. Generally, people respond in one of three ways when there is a fire in an organization:

- Ignore it and hope it goes away. (destructive)

- Ignite it by adding additional fuel such as their opinion. (destructive)

- Intervene with creative problem solving. (constructive)

Unfortunately, more and more ministry leaders, particularly pastors, find they are emotionally drained and outright exhausted because they are constantly fighting fires. Just as soon as one fire is out another ignites somewhere else in the organization. Not only is constant firefighting emotionally exhausting, but each fire has the potential to destroy everything you've worked so hard

...organizational fires always involve people and how leaders respond to fires always determines the damage done.

to achieve up to this point. It seems as though you are left with two options: (1) do nothing and risk everything or (2) continue fighting fires to save the organization while you lose your joy and get *burned-out* in the process.

I refuse to believe God wants you spending all your time or wasting your gifting only to say at the end of your life "I fought the *good* fire I kept the faith". While fires can be beneficial I don't think either option are what God has in mind for you.

The Bible is clear that fire is both a refiner and a revealer. If our works are motivated by selfishness or other impurities fire reveals it. How you may ask? You see, fire burns up works that are of inferior quality such as wood and straw; afterwards leaving behind nothing of lasting value. However, if our works are of eternal value, God allows fire to purify them and they become easily distinguishable as valuable to Him and others.

This is clearly seen in the refining process of precious metals such as gold. As the fire intensifies, the dross rises to the top and the gold is both distinguished and refined in the process. This only increases its worth and value. Ultimately, this means that fire can actually be a good thing in our lives and in our organizations. However, continual organizational fires may reveal competing values exist within your organization.

> **I refuse to believe God wants you spending all your time or wasting your gifting only to say at the end of your life "I fought the good fire I kept the faith".**

Wherever you have competing values, agendas, and motives you will always have continued conflict. The epistle of James makes it real plain.

But if you have bitter envy and self-seeking in your hearts... for where envy and self-seeking exist, confu- sion and every evil thing are there. James 3:14-16NKJV.

Where do wars and fights come from among you? Do they not come from your desires for pleasure that war in you members? You lust and do not have...you fight and war. James 4:1-2 NKJV

A FLAME RESISTANT CULTURE

So how do you change a church or organization where fighting, competition, envy, and continued conflict are the norm? As a church leadership consultant, I am asked this very question quite often. My answer is always the same. You build a flame resistant culture. Like a fireman's suit, a flame resistant culture covers and protects your organization from the devastation fires bring.

In fact, one of your greatest assignments as an organizational leader is creating a culture where people can grow and be all

God created them to be. This holds true for Christian leaders in both marketplace and ministry contexts. This is particularly true for pastors, also referred to as shepherds in scripture.

Shepherds lead, feed, guide, and protect their sheep. Some of you are marketplace entrepreneurial pastors. While your gift of shepherding is expressed outside of the church building and your sheep may be clients, customers, or employees you are still pastoring people.

David spent a lot of time around sheep before declaring in Palms 23, "The Lord is my shepherd, I shall not want. He makes me lie down in green pastures..." David knew that sheep only lie down, in green pastures, when three conditions are met.

IF YOU WANT THEM TO STAY
THEY MUST FIRST LAY

First sheep must be fully satisfied, not hungry before they lie down. A sheep lying down in the midst of grazing green pastures is like you and I lying down on Thanksgiving Day in front of a huge spread. That ain't happening at least not until after we're full! It's the same thing for sheep. Sheep must be fully satisfied before lying down in "green pastures".

Secondly, sheep will not lie down while there is conflict in their fold. If a sheep is at odds with another sheep it will remain standing on all fours. Essentially, the sheep remains on its feet and on its guard. This is why a culture of minimal conflict is necessary for the long-term development and health of any group of people. Without it, people remain closed, guarded and on their feet. In this position, like sheep, people (congregants, constituents, customers) are more likely to drift away, run away, or at minimum be distracted.

Finally, prior to lying down, sheep must feel the protection of their shepherd against any possible or pending outside enemy attack. What's most important here is that David recognizes his Shepherd (leader) as the one who leads him beside the *quite* waters, restores his soul, and thereby makes him lie down in green pastures. In other words, it is the shepherd's responsibility to ensure the right conditions exist for their sheep to lie down so their soul can be restored. Can you imagine your church being a place where people feel *compelled* to stay? The pastor, entrepreneur, or local business woman who creates this type of environment will reap the harvest of a loyal longterm following.

> **Eventually people will move on to a place where they can lie down if you don't create it for them.**

It could be argued that the most important duty a shepherd has is creating a safe place where sheep can feed and ultimately have their soul restored. While it's easy for pastors to focus on feeding the sheep (preaching and teaching) we must not overlook our leadership obligation to create a safe place where sheep can let their guard down, lie down, and be restored. This can't happen where there is constant conflict. In fact, overtime the grass will look greener on the other side. Eventually people will move on to a place where they can lie down if you don't create it for them. The good news is once you create such a place as a shepherd you also get to exhale.

When my kids get along it takes a lot of stress off of my wife and me. When they are at peace with each other we all get to relax. Therefore, it behooves me to proactively do all that I can to minimize conflict in my house.

You may be thinking, that is easier said than done. You are right. I guess if it were easier more people would do it. However, great leaders see new challenges as new chances for obtaining greater impact and amazing results. Sure, changing the culture of your home, company, or even your church is not an easy job; but, it is both doable and certainly worth it.

WHAT DOES A FLAME RESISTANT CULTURE LOOK LIKE?

Like a blanket, a flame resistant culture covers the people within your organization, family, or church. Flame resistant does not mean you'll never have a fire but it certainly minimizes the chances of having one and the damages you incur. Creating a fire-resistant culture takes intentionality, time, and consistent effort.

A great example of a fire-resistant culture is financial Guru Dave Ramsey's organization. Dave and his leaders have weaved some fire-resistant substances into their organization. One material can be summed up in a simple sentence, "spread praise around and send concerns up". This simply means that positive information and affirmation should move in every direction throughout his organization. However, complaints and concerns should be directed upwards where people have authority to appropriately address them.

Dave's employees don't gossip in the break room about things they don't like. They don't engage in negative side conversations at the water cooler. There are no after work meetings to discuss work-related "concerns". No, "I need you to pray about xyz," which is really gossip. Why? It's not in their organizational culture to do that. Instead, they direct their concerns to those above them who actually can solve them. Dave's people understand that complaints about either people or processes should be directed upwards. Now that's a novel idea!

You see, Dave took the time to articulate his vision and the organization's values upfront. (We'll talk more about values later). By doing this, he made his organization fire resistant. When a fire could break out it is easily recognized and quickly extinguished.

Newer employees quickly pick up on the culture and act in

ways that are appropriate. This eliminates the whispers and conversations that kill team and organizational morale. It also creates a fire-resistant culture where people grow and enjoy their time and work together.

Studies show people are far more productive when they enjoy both their work and those they work with. Additionally, they remain with their organization longer. Effective leaders create an atmosphere for both of these conditions to exist as the rule and not the exception.

2

FIREFIGHTERS:
Positioned To Protect

Dr. Samuel R. Chand

A few years ago, I was heating some oil in a frying pan before cooking. I left the pan on the burner and went into my backyard forgetting all about it. Fortunately, I returned to the house just in time. Just in time to see the oil in the frying pan in flames—8 to10 inch high flames.

Panicked I picked up the blazing frying pan, rushed it to the sink, and turned on the faucet. In the process, some flaming oil spilled on the kitchen floor and began to burn. At the same time the fire in the frying pan under the faucet was not dying down, but rather increasing. With the frying pan now in hand, I rushed through the patio door and dumped the flames on the grass. Now, I had two fires—the kitchen floor on the inside and a grass fire on the outside.

Inside first, I thought. So, I dumped the frying pan outside and proceeded to stomp out the fire on the kitchen floor. Yes, stomped out—I mean with my feet (I had shoes on). Stop laughing. Then I rushed back outside and hosed that fire out.

Try having to explain to your wife and kids that this was the final episode of *Cooking Gone Bad*. It was expensive too. The most expensive words are—"while we're at it". So, while we were at it, the whole kitchen got a makeover. Well beyond what we received from our insurance company.

Another time, right after we were married my wife and I left a couple foam pillows lying on top of base-board electric heaters in our apartment and went out to eat. When we returned and opened the door billows of smoke greeted us. We stumbled back down the stairs and rushed to the apartment manager's office to call the fire station. These were pre cell phone and 911 days.

Identify the cause of the fire—intentional or accidental.

The fire truck arrived and they carried out the two wimpy culprits (pillows) and set out ventilating fans to clear the apartment of smoke.

It was then we discovered the value of renter's insurance. We had none! We also discovered that smoke can permeate everything. So, with no insurance and no money (we were newly married kids who stayed broke) we had to have everything (drapes, clothes, furnishings) professionally cleaned and desmoked.

Identify your pyromaniacs.

Our pastor allowed us to spend the night in their home. We smelt of smoke from the episode with no clothes to change into (remember broke). As a humorous aside, the next morning we all went out to breakfast still smelling like a smoke stack and the person seating us asked, "Smoking or Non-Smoking". We lost it then!

So, I've had a little experience with house fires. I am always amazed at firefighters. As first responders they run to the fire while the rest of us run from the fire. Firefighters are well trained and equipped to fight fires. However, they are responders. They wait for the call. Once the call is in they are on their way. Timing is also critical

> **Call for help and do it quickly.**

in firefighting. Minutes and seconds count. Being notified of a fire in a timely manner makes a huge difference.

Then there are degrees of fires. Some can be handled in house for others we call 911. Knowing this difference can be crucial. This can make the difference between saving your house or it ending up in ashes. How fires start is a critical factor. Some are accidental human errors or negligence, while others are started by lightening or intentional lighting.

Good news and bad news. The bad news—fires cannot be avoided. The good news is that fires can be contained and often preempted.

California is famous for its devastating and massive fires. While hundreds of firefighters are pouring water and other fire-retarding chemicals from land and air there are others who don't have a hose in their hands—they have shovels. With these shovels

> **People say that most organizational fires start amidst change—not true.**

they are digging a trench outside the fire's perimeter to contain the fire. Amazingly, sometimes these very firefighters will intentionally start fires outside the fire's perimeter to burn out an area so that the oncoming fire will not have anything to burn. At other times minimizing oxygen to the fire removes the fuel needed by the fire to rage.

All the readers of this chapter who are leaders are already drawing principles from the preceding paragraphs. I'll get you started and would love to hear back from you (www.samchand. com) on additional principles.

- Identify the cause of the fire—intentional or accidental. This is important so we will know whether to deal with the "what" or "who". Intentional fire setting and accidental fires have vastly differing ramifications.

- Identify your pyromaniacs. Every organization is blessed with at least one. These are people who are always tinkering with matches near the gas can. They are offensive, abrasive and careless people who throw around their position, words, and other object with no thought of the fall out and the fires they cause. You will find yourself putting out fires they start.

Watch the back burner issues. They are smoldering.

- Call for help and do it quickly. Regardless if the fire is intentional or accidental you need to call for help. Who's on your 911 list to call? In the event of an organizational fire do you have a short list of first responders to call?

- If your leadership calls for frequent firefighting, create a team. Teams can do much more than individuals. Teams can expose causes of frequent fires, deploy for special assignments, and develop as specialists in certain fires.

- People say that most organizational fires start amidst change—not true. Most organizational fires start in transition. Change is the event while transition involves the emotional, relational, financial, logistical and other component before, during, and after change.

Sometimes you just have to let the fire run its course and burn itself out.

- Strategically deploy your firefighters. If you watch the Sunday morning talk shows on TV you will notice firefighting. Firefighters are deployed by political parties, the White House, special interest groups and others to either smother a fire, start a fire, or say there is no fire.

Words cause more fires...

- Build trust and respect by giving and receiving the same.

- Whatever is left on the back burner will burn sooner or later. Watch the back burner issues. They are smoldering.

- Remove as much fuel from the fire as possible so it can smother and suffocate itself.

- Sometimes you just have to let the fire run its course and burn itself out.

- Words cause more fires than all the matches and cooking oil in the frying pan can.

> James 3:5-6 (New International Version) [5]Likewise the tongue is a small part of the body, but it makes great boasts. Consider what a great forest is set on fire by a small spark. [6]The tongue also is a fire, a world of evil among the parts of the body. It corrupts the whole person, sets the whole course of his life on fire, and is itself set on fire by hell.

> James 3:5-6 (The Message) [5]A word out of your mouth may seem of no account, but it can accomplish nearly anything—or destroy it! [6]It only takes a spark, remember, to set off a forest fire. A careless or wrongly placed word out of your

mouth can do that. By our speech we can ruin the world, turn harmony to chaos, throw mud on a reputation, send the whole world up in smoke and go up in smoke with it, smoke right from the pit of hell.

3

EARTHQUAKES:
When Values Collide

Dr. Don Brawley III

*We do not act rightly because we have virtue or excellence,
but we rather have those because we have acted rightly.*

~ Aristotle

Over the past several years, a relatively unknown Bible personality has gained a lot of attention in movies. Her name is Mary, Mary Magdalene. Secular screen writers have made many assumptions about her life. I'd argue they aren't true and the little we actually know of her is found in scripture.

On one occasion Mary Magdalene broke her alabaster box and used the precious oil it contained to anoint the body of Jesus. This act was one of love, self-denial, and faith. You see, the oil that quickly flowed out of it was the equivalent of one year's salary. To answer Tina Turner, love has everything to do with it!

Moreover, it proved Mary trusted God for her future since along with losing the alabaster box Mary likely gave up any hope of being married.

Marriage to a Jewish maiden was of enormous importance
and consequence. Jewish culture

> **When people don't
> have shared values their
> organization experiences
> regular tremors and
> haphazard quakes.**

valued the marriage relationship,
the home, and the family as life's
greatest treasures. The dowry was
essential to marriage. Mary's gift
may very well have cost her the
right to marry. This gift may very
well have represented her dreams as far as husband, children,
and family were concerned. [1]

Jesus was impressed by her act. Judaist Iscariot was upset. On
the surface it appeared he was angry because the oil could have
been sold and used for the poor. Mary's worship and Judaist's
words caused a shake that day.

Surely everyone in the room felt the shaking too. The shake was
great enough for Jesus to stop what he was doing and publicly
address it. This is an excellent example of how people's values
collide and cause tremors. What happened beyond the obvious?

On the surface it may appear to be a difference in how
money would be allocated. Yet, a closer look reveals it was
actually unseen *values plates* colliding with each other. Mary
Magdalene's choice proved she loved Jesus and demonstrated
her gratefulness for His forgiveness. What about Judaist
Iscariot? Jesus said it wasn't that he *cared* for the poor, but that
he was a thief. While Mary valued her savior Judaist valued
himself.

WHAT'S DRIVING YOU?

Values drive human behavior. They influence your thoughts,
feelings, and actions. In general, every decision and every
action you make is driven by a personal value. This is true when
you are aware of it and when you are not. The same holds true
in organizations.

Values are the enduring virtues you build your organization on. They are the non-negotiables that provide fuel for your vision, direction for decision-making, simplify choices, and drive behaviors. When key stakeholders share values things operate smoothly, people enjoy working together, and goals are achieved.

It's not hard to make decisions

when you know what your values are.

~ Roy Disney

When people don't have shared values their organization experiences regular tremors and haphazard quakes. Just like earthquakes occur when non-visible plates collide below the earth's surface so do organizational quakes. Like physical earthquakes, the effects of values colliding are often very costly, far reaching, and enduring.

You may be experiencing some shakin' right now. Perhaps you thought it was simply a difference in opinion. Maybe you didn't understand why someone got so emotional about their blocked goal. Perhaps a whole group of people left your ministry because of one seemingly small difference. Perhaps you are new in your leadership position and wonder why every time you attempt to lead your people in a specific direction the ground shakes beneath your feet.

First, let me say you are not crazy. I consult ministry and marketplace leaders all the time who share your feelings of frustration and weariness. Nothing is more draining than rowing your boat north while those behind you row south! You can rediscover the joy, freedom, and results that occur when everyone rows in the same direction.

Second, don't let people drive you crazy!

Third, don't let people drive you crazy! That was worth saying twice!

My guess is the shaking you are experiencing isn't as simple as a difference in opinion; rather, it is opposing values colliding. Here are just a few *typical* plates that often collide in churches:

Group A: "I don't think we should be singing all that contemporary stuff. I like to sing the songs we grew up on."

Group B: "How are we going to reach the next generation if all we sing are songs that were written centuries ago?"

Values colliding: traditional verses contemporary

Revealing question: How do we define traditional and contemporary? (Note: most hymns were thought of as too contemporary during the generation they were written).

Group A: "Why does the pastor spend so much time with the new people? It's like he forgot us. After all, if it weren't for us we wouldn't even have a church today."

Group B: "We need to make our first time guests feel comfortable and relaxed. We want them to enjoy their time with us. Perhaps they will join our church family."

Values colliding: growth versus decline, natives versus new comers, service versus "serve-us"

Revealing question: Who will be our church's ministry priority?

Group A: "What ever happened to calling me and telling me that we have a meeting? Everyone is e-mailing and texting these days. I don't think I can get with that. That's almost worst than the PowerPoint with the songs on it being in the sanctuary."

Group B: "I love being able to see the words to the songs on PowerPoint. I can participate more in the praise and worship service without having to mouth the words. I also like the translation pastor has been using lately. I never really understood all that 'thee' and 'thou' stuff."

Values colliding: innovation versus stagnation.

Revealing question: What is the church? Is the church the steeple (building) or the people?

Don't feel bad. This is not uncommon in any organization. You see, people who join your church and connect with your organization bring all of them when they come. They bring their past experiences, longstanding belief systems, personal desires, and aspirations. Often a person's personal values are not totally in alignment with the organization's values.

BUILDING YOUR HOUSE

Think about Habitat for Humanity International. They are known for their benevolence typically seen as they build houses for the less fortunate. When people volunteer their time, talent, and treasure to build someone a house you never hear any volunteer say, "Why don't we get paid for all this work we are doing?" There is a reason why you would never hear this type of language.

When a person volunteers for Habitat for Humanity they are clear

> **...people will always come and go in and out of your church.**

about the organization's mission, values, and philosophy. Habitat is a *not for profit* organization devoted to building "simple, decent and affordable housing" with the use of volunteer labor. When volunteers show up they don't expect to be served nor do they expect to be paid. The new homeowner participates in building the house too. The general rule of thumb is the homeowner is expected to put in 500 hundred hours of sweat equity. The new homeowner and all volunteers know Habitat values volunteer service and benevolence.

My guess is they will never have as much as a tremor about who they serve and how they serve. No matter how much money is offered everyone already knows they are not for profit. They have clarified their values and developed a strong culture over time. Doing so keeps riff raft out. Even more importantly it determines who comes in.

You see people will always come and go in and out of your church. However, when you create shared values YOU get to decide which ones you keep! Those that don't share your values either won't come at all or won't last long. This is good for all parties involved. Those that don't fit can find a church better suited for them. As a result, you attract people who truly connect with what you and your church are all about. Over time, like Habitat for Humanity, you will have a strong and healthy organization.

Benefits of creating shared values:

- Unifies efforts

- Clarifies direction

- Simplifies decision-making

- Prioritizes actions

- Communicates what's important

- Attracts others with similar values

- Weeds out others with opposing values before they join.

SHAKE THEM OUT BEFORE THEY SHAKE YOU DOWN

The best place to tackle these issues is before people join. Let them know what you stand for before they join. Often churches spend a lot of time going over their beliefs, creeds, and basic Biblical foundational issues. I have found that this is not the best use of time for new people who are being assimilated into a new organization.

People rarely leave a church because of its beliefs or even the pastor's sermon. Generally, they leave because of a difference in opinion regarding the church's strategy which is derived from its values and vision. This is not to say, Bible foundations and creeds aren't important. They are. However, these items can be taught in depth *after* the individual determines if they even fit in your church at all.

Assimilating people into your church and training them on your beliefs first is like adopting a new pet into your family that you are allergic to. Please note, I am not reducing people to pets, but am trying to illustrate a point. You know it's only a matter of time before you have to find the pet another home, so why would you spend weeks and months house training the pet if they ultimately won't or can't stay? Frankly, you are wasting their time and yours while moving opposing plates towards each other.

Are you saying turn away someone because they have different values than your church? Absolutely not. I am saying you need to clarify your values and allow people the option of making an informed decision, prior to joining, to see if they fit there or not.

This should be done upfront, perhaps in a new member 's class or orientation. If you don't do this upfront it will be done later. Later is usually after the shake, quake, and damage have already been done.

If a person doesn't join your church or organization because of what you value it is actually a good thing. It means you just saved yourself a whole lot of trouble down road. Remember, there are different types of churches each capable of serving different people. Your church is not called to reach everyone.

If we aren't willing to pay a price for our values,
then we should ask ourselves whether
we truly believe in them at all.

~ Barack Obama

WHEN THE BIG ONE STRIKES

I grew up in the suburbs of New York City on Long Island. Long Island is a literal island having water on all four sides. Both Brooklyn and Queens are on Long Island's most western parts. I grew up in Suffolk County which runs from about the middle of Long Island to its most eastern point.

I remember watching the news back in the early eighties one night after a small tremor rattled our area. The media acknowledged the tremor and how it measured on the Richter scale. Then the real news came.

Long Island has a fault that runs north and south nearly through the middle of it. It literally divides the island into east and west. That was news to me. Even worse, was the fact that geologist expected the "big one" to eventually strike and sever Eastern Long Island. They predict one day Eastern Long Island will fall off into the ocean. Guess what side we lived on? You guessed right, the East side.

Actually, our house was either on the East side or directly on the fault line. That translates this way. Best case scenario we'd be washed out to sea with the rest of the island. Worst case scenario, our house would crumble into the shifting plates below the fault line. Somehow neither option seemed very appealing then nor do they now.

I always knew it wasn't a question of if, but when the big one would strike. As long as there were non-aligned shifting plates beneath the surface a split would occur one day. Thereafter, every tremor reminded me that the big one would eventually come. The same can be said of your church when opposing values exist.

THE GREAT DIVIDE

Often in a church setting, you know when the big one has struck because the church splits. I don't know of any other clearer and more visible sign of values colliding than a church splitting. Unfortunately, this happens more than any of us would like to think or admit. I can say that I've been part of a church split before and the pain that it engenders is not easily forgotten. Often it lingers over years as:

• Feelings of disloyalty abound and a lack of trust increases.

• Long-term relationships are broken.

- People are forced to choose sides.

- Church morale sinks into an all-time low.

- Family members split as one part stays and the other goes with the new church.

- Competition wages between the original church and new church members as each feel compelled to prove "God is with us" and on our side.

- Phones ring and people whisper in the parking lot about the latest happenings.

- The first church struggles to recover from its loss of talent and treasure.

...how do I know if there are competing values in my organization? I'd say look real closely at your leadership.

Unfortunately, this type of quake can hit any church no matter how small, large, young, old, or where it's located. Sadly, I've seen it happen time and time again. After it strikes, I've been called in to help rebuild the ruins. Fortunately, you don't have to sit back and just wait for the big one. There are better alternatives we'll consider in a moment.

You may wonder, how do I know if there are competing values in my organization? I'd say look real closely at your leadership.

- Is everyone on the same page?

- Do all key stakeholders have unity on what you stand for?

- Are leaders' behaviors consistent with your organization's values?

- Is there a group of people, who share some type of

affinity, pulling in a totally different direction than everyone else?

- Is there any leader(s) that seems like a magnet for others that do not uphold your values? (This is a big indicator).

- Do leaders uphold agreed upon standards when the senior leader is not present?

- Are your leaders more loyal to you or your vision?

Splits only come through leadership. I need to repeat that. It is highly unlikely that your congregation will cause a split. In general, only a leader can. Members may cause some tremors; however, only leaders bring on the big one. Remember in crises and change people look to leaders for direction. In this scenario only a leader (formal or informal) would be received enough to be followed and thus cause a split.

YOU ARE CLOSER TO A QUAKE THAN BEFORE

While you may see the value in what we've discussed perhaps you don't see its relevance with contemporary leadership. I'd like to take a moment and tie the two together. I believe it will all make sense in a moment.

As stated earlier we are living in a time of dramatic, swift, and ongoing change. Our society is changing faster than ever before. Additionally, for the first time in our history we have four different generations all in the same workplace at the same time. Each generation values something different than the others. At times what they value is in stark contrast to those in another generation.

For instance, the Builders Generation (those born before 1945) value sacrifice while Busters (those born between 1965-1980) value balance. You can see how a Builder could easily be frustrated by a Buster who never "sacrifices" to get the job done. You can also see how a Buster could feel infringed upon when asked to "sacrifice" extra time to serve. She might feel like doing so would take her out of "balance". Of course, this sounds crazy to the Builder because when she grew up, "we always came together to make sure everything was done at the church". However, the Buster works a full-time job and juggles a second one as a "soccer mom" for her children.

Remember I told you people bring their past experiences, belief systems, aspirations, and desires with them when they join. Well, they really do. The problem again is that each of us brings in different history and different angles by which we see the present. This is just one scenario of how generational differences can set off tremors in your organization.

There are plenty of other reasons why you are more susceptible to a values quake than ever before. However, I will only consider one other reason. Our nation is becoming more and more polarized. People are choosing sides and they are very much opposing to each other. The gray area is quickly becoming black or white. Either you:

- Are for gay marriage and thus against the traditional family or you are against it and considered a bigot.

- Believe there are many ways to God (inclusion) or you believe Jesus is the only way (exclusion).

- Are on the liberal left or the conservative right.

- Are a have or a have not (the middle class is shrinking).

WHERE DID THE MIDDLE GO?

More than ever, people are choosing sides and the middle is disappearing. This is different than before. In past times, most people were considered to be in the middle. Think of the bell curve you learned about in school (See Appendix). Most people were considered to be average and therefore fell into the middle. They were average height, had average grades, average income, average family size, and the list goes on. However, there seems to be a new trend emerging. It is reflected in the Well curve (See Appendix).

The Well curve is an inverted Bell curve. [2] In a Well curve most people gravitate towards extremities. Either you are on the left or the right, few are in the middle. You see this throughout society as:

- The Middle class is shrinking.

- Stores are getting larger and smaller. (Walmart and boutiques/speciality shops like Starbucks grow in popularity while medium sized companies like Sears and K-Mart decrease.)

- Televisions are getting larger and smaller. (Plazma, I-pod)

- People are eating healthier foods (organic) and more fast foods.

- People are more connected (internet) and more disconnected personally. (Often they are present but not there.)

- Americans increasingly prefer mega or micro-sized churches, but not mid-sized.

- New church goers are either very active or hardly active.

When people join your church or support your organization they bring societal thoughts and trends with them. Each has implications on how we lead them.

THE REASON BEHIND YOUR STORM

Recently, I heard the simplest yet most astounding reason behind every storm. It was put like this:

The reason for every hurricane is that water is out of alignment.

The reason for every tornado is wind out of alignment.

The reason for every earthquake is plates out of alignment.

You may be asking is that it? Yup, that's it. Well not quite.

Whenever something is out of alignment it naturally seeks alignment. This includes weather systems and even systems in your body. When the systems in your body are out of alignment we call it disease. Disease brings disease.

> **Whenever things are perfectly aligned doors of opportunity open.**

When weather systems are out of alignment we get earthquakes, hurricanes, tornados and other types of storms. However, when things are in alignment we feel good, the storms cease, and the quiet appears. Not only does alignment bring calm security and a sense of serene peace it also unlocks doors and releases potential.

Over twenty years ago, when I engaged my wife we noticed something very interesting. One day she was locked out of her house. My house key unlocked her house door. Naturally, I thought my brother's key would unlock her front door too since he and I had the same house key. Not so.

However, any time Mona didn't have her key I could open the door for her. Do you know why? It's because I have the key to her heart. While that is true, that's not why! It's because somehow my key was perfectly *aligned* with her lock.

Every locked door opens when alignment occurs. Whenever things are perfectly aligned doors of opportunity open. New possibilities appear. The reason you have been experiencing tremors is so you can see which plates are out of line. Then, overtime, you can regain alignment and walk into new opportunities.

HOW DO WE GET INTO ALIGNMENT?

First your family, church, or organization will need to determine what it stands for. This is a task of leadership, perhaps the first and most important one. In order for leaders to determine what their organization stands for, its **Leaders always clarify their own core values before those of their organization.** leaders must definitively know what they stand for personally. Leaders always clarify their own core values before those of their organization. After they do, they can determine and uphold the values of their organization with greater confidence and conviction.

Personal leadership is the process of
keeping your vision and values before you
and aligning your life to be congruent with them.

~ Stephen Covey

Secondly, leaders clarify their organization's core values. Core values declare the virtues most important to an organization. When these values are declared and shared they give tremendous credibility, power, and focus to the group that lives them. Moreover, they simplify decision-making and reduce conflict. All stake-owners agree on who the organization is thus making it easier to determine how it grows to its fullest potential.

Often conflict results from differences in the *how* and *what* because the *who* wasn't established, defined, and shared first. Organizations like individuals can only hold to a small number of core values. When people don't share values conflict inevitably is the result.

Finally, once you've declared and shared your organization's core values you'll need to ensure your firefighters, protectors of purpose, are in place.

I have oversimplified the process of creating shared values and changing organizational culture. It is neither quick nor easy, yet it is definitely possible and the benefits immeasurable.

Generally, Fortune 500 companies, school districts, and other organizations bring professionals in and allow them to do it for them. I can say it would be easier for you to do personally in a brand new organization than in an organization that has any history.

> **Often conflict results from differences in the *how* and *what* because the *who* wasn't established**

I can also say that it is one of the wisest investments you could ever make. Choosing to do so is probably the single most important decision you could ever make for your organization.

This is why Fortune 500 companies and other major organizations commit to the process and thereby enjoy longevity and success. Consider the following:

- Private owned companies like Chik-fil-A make more money in six days than their competitors do in seven and even recently boasted of a 10% gain for the first half of 2009 amid an economic downturn.

- I'm told the average tenure of Billy Graham's staff is over thirty years.

- While some airlines closed after 9/11 and others have laid-off employees, Southwest Airlines has never laid-off one person. What makes this company different from their competitors? Their leaders and employees know who they are, what they stand for, and all stakeholder have internalized their core values.

Creating shared values and a strong culture is not something I can tell you how to do in a book. It is something you have to be trained to do. It took me years to learn how to effectively do this. I *practiced* on the church I pastor (thank God it worked... whew) and now confidently walk alongside other pastors I consult as they do the same.

JUST A LITTLE ABOUT MY JOURNEY

My journey to become a Doctor of Strategic Leadership began when I became frustrated leading the church I pastored. Week after week people left encouraged, but I left discouraged. I didn't like who our church was becoming. I was unhealthy and so was our church. I'm ashamed to say that we were becoming personality driven. I hated it.

I didn't like the pressure it put on my family or me. Don't get me wrong. At first it was fun. I felt like I had a big "S" on my chest that stood for "Super pastor ". There I was again and again off to the rescue!

Over time that got real old and I got really tired. I didn't like people looking to me rather than God. Nor did I like living to meet their expectations rather than God's. Eventually I realized I carried a burden God never intended me to carry. Who could I blame though? After all, I didn't inherit the church. I was the one who planted it!

To make a long story short, I ended up formally studying organizational and strategic leadership for nearly seven years. During this time I saw our church completely transformed. As a result, I love the church I pastor today.

I'm glad to say I'm healthy and so is our church. No longer do people look to me, they look to God to meet their needs. Moreover, despite the current economic storm our church is nearly debt free and currently experiencing its highest year of giving in fifteen years. Most importantly, lives are being transformed and God glorified.

If your goal is to change the culture of any organization beyond your household I strongly encourage you to enlist the help of an expert. If you chose not to, you run the risk of mediocre results at best and irreparable damage at worst. Regardless, my purpose is to expose you to the reality that it can be done.

Additionally, I want you to see how it is the responsibility of leadership to create a culture that maximizes organizational performance and blesses all those who interact with the organization. Moreover, I hope you can envision how much more productive and effective everyone could be when values are shared. Finally, can you imagine how much more enjoyable your role would be if you actually got to function in it without the distraction and devastations associated with fires, tremors, and quakes?

NOTES

1. Generis Partners, LLC (2005) Minister 's Preaching Resource p. 25
2. IBM Institute for Business Value (2003). The Well Curve was described in the following artcle Pink, Daniel H. "The Shape of things to Come". Wired 2003

3

EARTHQUAKES:
When Values Collide

Dr. Samuel R. Chand

I have never been in an earthquake, but I have talked to people who have. They tell me it is a never to be forgotten experience. The tremors are in a variety of phases. There are the pre-tremors before the main event and then there are the post-tremors which can be as destructive. Here are some excerpts from Wikipedia…

An earthquake (also known as a tremor or temblor) is the result of a sudden release of energy in the Earth's crust that creates seismic waves. Earthquakes are recorded with a seismometer, also known as a seismograph. The moment magnitude of an earthquake is conventionally reported, or the related and mostly obsolete Richter magnitude, with magnitude 3 or lower earthquakes being mostly imperceptible and magnitude 7 causing serious damage over large areas. Intensity of shaking is measured on the modified Mercalli scale.

At the Earth's surface, earthquakes manifest themselves by shaking and sometimes displacing the ground. When a large earthquake epicenter is located offshore, the seabed sometimes suffers sufficient dis- placement to cause a tsunami. The shaking in earthquakes can also trigger landslides and occasionally volcanic activity.

The term epicenter refers to the point at ground level directly above the hypocenter.

Here are a number of afterthoughts…

- Earthquakes are internal. They start on the inside and manifest themselves on the outside. Watch what is going on internally in your organization because it will manifest itself externally. Efficiency leads to effectiveness. Efficiency is the internal functioning of the organization. Effectiveness is the external manifestation of the organization. Most organizations focus their efforts on the effectiveness not realizing that its genesis is in the internal efficiency.

> **Be sure to know the fault lines or fault people in your organization. It will happen.**

Internal customer/member service will lead to better external customer/member service.

People treat others how they are treated.

- While the timing of the earthquake might not be predictable, the eventuality and inevitability is. Be sure to know the fault lines or fault people in your organization. It will happen. Aren't you encouraged?

- Earthquakes can be measured. You too can measure the degree to which an earthquake has affected you. Why is that important? Because not every earthquake needs the same response. Some wise sage once observed—don't use a sledgehammer to kill a fly when a swatter will

> **…not every earthquake needs the same response.**

do. Most people over react and treat all earthquakes as the same. They are not.

- The epicenter needs the most attention—that is where the greatest concentrated damage takes place When responding to an earthquake quickly discovering and respond- ing to the epicenter could mean the difference between survival and demise. In an organization, the epicenter will usually be a person camouflaged as a department. Deal with your epicenter.

> **In an organization, the epicenter will usually be a person camouflaged as a department.**

- An earthquake happens when two incongruent land masses collide underground. In my consulting work with high-impact, world-class leaders I have discovered where the incongruence lies.

My consultation with senior leaders has altered much over time. I used to do much more organizationally oriented work. Now, I focus most of my attention on the primary leader. I have found three areas that need congruence without which "fault lines" will be formed deep within the leader.

> **Don't be an earthquake waiting to happen.**

1. **The person** as a man/woman, husband/wife, father/ mother—the being.

2. **The leader** of the organization regardless of the nature of work.

3. **The visionary** who wants to do much more beyond the present role in the organization—the dreamer.

You're all three. These three primary components of a person have to be recognized and organized to avert an earthquake.

How congruent are you?

How do you get and keep alignment in all three spheres?

Who is helping you to discover, develop, and deploy?

Don't be an earthquake waiting to happen.

4

DAMAGE CONTROL:
The Leader and His Relationships

Dr. Don Brawley III

A loving relationship is one in which the loved one is free to be himself - to laugh with me, but never at me; to cry with me, but never because of me; to love life, to love himself, to love being loved. Such a relationship is based upon freedom and can never grow in a jealous heart.

~ Leo F. Buscaglia

FIREPROOF: NEVER LEAVE YOUR PARTNER BEHIND

Recently, Kirk Cameron stared in the Christian themed movie, *Fireproof: Never Leave your Partner Behind.* Fireproof tells the story of a young married couple whose lives drift apart. Both the husband (Cameron) and wife's actions seemed to constantly rub each other the wrong way. Slammed doors, penetrating silence, and disregard for one another became commonplace in their relationship.

Cameron played a firefighter who would eventually learn the value of fighting for his marriage despite the heat. Over time, Cameron learned his passion for boating and even his job as a firefighter were secondary to his relationship with his spouse. By the movie's end, his efforts paid off and the ashes of a ruined marriage faded into the distance as something stronger emerged.

The movie effectively depicted the commitment and work it takes to have long-lasting and more fulfilling relationships. However, there are exceptions to lifelong relationships. There are some people you have partnered with yesterday, yet God is allowing today's fire to burn the ties that bind you!

There are people that you must let go of. In fact, your future and all those who journey with you depends on both those you retain and those you release. If you hold on to where God was you inevitably forfeit where He is today and is ultimately leading you tomorrow. While some people were a good fit yesterday not all of them are a good fit for you today.

> **...your future and all those who journey with you depends on both those you retain and those you release.**

Some people have served their purpose in your life and vice-versa. Once you become aware of this the most loving thing you can do for the other party is release him. I do not mean simply "cut them off", but lovingly release them to connect with the person(s) that God has ordained for this time in their life.

You will bless them in ways they can't begin to fully appreciate now. Meanwhile you will free yourself and your team from unnecessary heartache. Like Jonah joined himself with people going opposite of his call and thereby caused them an unnecessary storm these people will challenge you with needless storms as long as they remain on board.

There is a well known expression that, often in hindsight, helps us make sense of the relationships in our lives. You know it.

Some people come into our lives for a reason, a season, and others a lifetime. Unlike the loaf of bread you bought from the store the other day relationships don't have a "best if used by" date although often they have an unknown "shelf-life". This means you'll have to rely on what you sense in your spirit, your knower, to determine when the relationship has expired.

Now, let me be clear. Some relationships are just not optional. For instance, your spouse should be on your lifetime list! However, there are other relationships that become toxic particularly when they are allowed to continue beyond their time or purpose. Unfortunately, often we have a hard time determining who belongs in which category until after the damage is done.

YOU CAN'T SAVE EVERYBODY

Before I continue, I want to tell you about Ella. Ella was a dear friend of mine when she was in high school and I was in junior high. We were both believers when we met although we went to different churches. Ella was an older woman, about sixteen, had a license and a car. So of course I didn't mind hanging out with her!

One particular summer, Ella went on a retreat with some youth from her church. Everyone was having a great time when they realized it was time to return home. Not really ready to leave, the group decided to go canoeing one more time before they pulled out. So off they went.

Just prior to returning to shore, Ella's canoe capsized and she and her partner fell into the lake. The water was deep above their heads and Ella didn't know how to swim. Like anyone drowning, she panicked. The young man in her canoe knew how to swim and attempted to save her. Unfortunately, Ella, in desperate fear, fought so hard that she drowned that day.

Although I knew she was with the Lord, I'll never forget how sad I was when I heard the news.

Even worst, not only did Ella die, but the young man who knew how to swim died while trying to save her. Although his efforts were certainly heroic ultimately they were in vain. Ella was strong willed anyway and that only increased with her understandable state of panic. The young man did

...toxic relationships will kill you if you don't relinquish their hold first.

his best to save her but could not. When he realized he could not it was too late, she would not let him go. I'm sure he thought he could save her before he lost his life attempting to do so.

Like Ella's canoe partner, we too are tempted to "save" people we can't. Some people fight so hard against being helped till they place your future and ultimately your life in harm's way. Often by the time you realize it, they have a hold on you that makes it either too complicated to untangle or deathly threatening to your immediate future. These toxic relationships will kill you if you don't relinquish their hold first. To do so, requires both courage and perception.

As a leader, you must develop your perception muscles and recognize when things are going south before they actually do. Doing so reduces the personal and organizational fallout often experienced when we overstay in relationships. I use the terminology *perception muscle* for two reasons.

First, there isn't a science or methodology for determining how long people should hold specific spaces in our lives. Not only, do people fill *places* (roles) in our lives, they also fill *spaces* of intimacy. Some spaces are more intimate than others, while other spaces are more formal and perhaps even more distant.

Dr. A. R. Bernard taught this valuable lesson at a conference I attended many years ago. Whenever people fill spaces they are not mature enough to fill, we allow them to stay beyond their appointed time, or they take the space casually they inevitably trespass.

KEEP OUT—NO TRESPASSING ALLOWED!

To trespass is to enter into territory that is either off limits or simply reserved for someone else. Essentially, trespassing is when people enter spaces of our lives they have not been authorized to enter. While the place a person has in our life involves their role, the space they fill considers the level of *intimacy shared.*

It has been said that intimacy can be best described as "into-me-you-see". Essentially, intimacy involves the spatial proximity a person possesses relative to your heart. When a person of the opposite gender is given too close of a space in a

> **...the *place* a person has in our life involves their role, the *space* they fill considers the level of *intimacy* shared.**

leader 's life the leader may enter into an *emotional* affair. This relatively new terminology applies to a married person who has an "affair of the heart".

When a man or woman has an emotional affair someone else possesses their spouse's *space*. Think of it like a reserved parking space. As long as someone is parked in that space no one else can park there, not even a person's spouse. This means the individual's spouse has to find a different and more distant parking space. You see, unlike roles which can be filled by a multitude of people, only one person can fill a particular space in your life at a time.

Emotional affairs are always dangerous and usually disastrous. While emotional affairs don't always lead to sexual affairs, often they do. Studies show that over 50% of sexual affairs start on the job. In this context, generally a man falls for a woman who *admires* him and a woman for a man who is *attentive* to her inner needs.

> ...unlike roles which can be filled by a multitude of people, only one person can fill a particular space in your life at a time.

For instance, a male pastor may have a female secretary. Her role is clearly understood by her title and detailed in her job description. However, if the pastor begins sharing his deepest ministry or marriage hurts with her he inevitably puts her in an inappropriate space. Of course, the opposite applies here as well.

The pastor's secretary may inappropriately divulge deep areas of her personal life with the pastor. Before long, the two begin having a relationship of the heart. Unfortunately, what they easily lose sight of is that doing so will likely cause great devastation for both parties in the very near future.

LOOK A LITTLE CLOSER

We see this happen all the time. Lately, we've really seen a lot of this within the political arena. The public apologies all begin the same way. It starts with something like, "I'm sorry for all the pain I caused my wife, children, staff, constituents, etc... It started very innocently..." In many cases this may be true as affairs generally don't start with a sexual act, but a *spatial act.*

Typically, a leader allows someone with a role in his life to fill the wrong space in his life. This is one of many reasons why leadership should start at home. No matter how seemingly successful a leader appears in public, it is his or her private life that ultimately determines public success. This means leaders must make every effort to fortify their personal and family *lives* first. Doing so prevents marketplace and ministry disasters. Not doing so may ultimately bring trespassing and transgression.

While emotional and sexual affairs are extremely dangerous, trespassing is not limited to just those situations. People trespass every time they go into unauthorized territory in your life. This is clearly seen whenever (a) you notice a person *continually* being offended by you

No matter how seemingly successful a leader appears in public, it is his or her private life that ultimately determines public success.

or (b) a person's actions repeatedly offends you. Both scenarios are indicators that the person is likely in the wrong space. He is probably too close. Often this is seen when a person:

- Disrespects you.

- Reduces your *leadership* role in their life and follows you *arbitrarily*.

- Becomes too *familiar* with you and thereby takes your role in his life *casually*.

Do not confuse toxic relationships or even trespassing with the much needed toil that builds solid enduring relationships. We are not in heaven yet; therefore, our relationships will cause some degree of hurt, disappointment, and will require a lot of work. This is because two imperfect people can never have a perfect relationship, but they can mature as they grow together.

The meeting of two personalities is like
the contact of two chemical substances:
if there is any reaction, both are transformed.

~ Carl Jung

In general though, whenever a person consistently trespasses it shows he is in the wrong space in your life. It is unloving for you to keep a person in a space they cannot handle. Jesus' example shows leaders have the responsibility of ensuring others are lovingly placed in spaces where minimum trespassing occurs.

PUT THEM IN THEIR SPACE

Jesus was a master at keeping people in their space. Take a quick look at the disciples. John was the disciple "Jesus loved". Essentially, the two were very close in heart. It was not unusual to see John leaning on Jesus breast. This exemplifies the intimate relationship the two men shared. Also, notice John is the disciple Jesus left his mother 's care to as he prepared to return to heaven. John held a very close space in Jesus' life. Peter had a different space as did James and even Judaist Iscariot. As a leader, you will have to monitor and manage who fills the spaces in your life. Often this means staying flexible and fluid in how you relate with others.

Keep in mind that just because a person has handled a specific space in the past doesn't mean they can today. The opposite is also true. Just because someone in the past was unable to fill a particular space yesterday does not necessarily mean they can't today. Why?

Nothing on this side of heaven stays the same except change. You have changed in big and small ways over time. Similarly, the other person has changed too. Resultantly, relationships are dynamic, fluid, and always evolving and changing. This means you must prayerfully protect the spaces in your life and lovingly reposition people accordingly. Sometimes this means bringing a person in closer. Other times you'll have to create a greater spatial distance between you and the individual.

Sometimes when you make these adjustments, you will need to explain what you're doing. Doing so ensures the other party understands. This is particularly true when you are making a major spatial adjustment which involves changing roles too.

For instance, perhaps an employee has been directly answering to you; however, you need to put more space (distance) in that relationship. You may decide to allow that employee to answer to someone else. In that case, you'll probably need to explain

...we always teach others how to treat us.

what has changed, possibly why it has changed, and your new expectations. More than not though, these adjustments will go unspoken.

You don't always have to change the spaces people fill in formal ways. You don't have to call a board meeting or have a conference call each time an adjustment is made. In general, as you change by repositioning *yourself* people *relearn* how to treat you and where (in a spatial sense) to meet you.

> *Be good to yourself. People will only treat*
> *you as well as you treat yourself.*
>
> ~ Mark Victor Hansen

You will quickly find that it's easier to change yourself than it is to change the multitude of people in your sphere of influence. As you change yourself others around you inevitably change. Why? Because relationships are all about *how* people *relate* with each other. Whenever you move or change in how you relate with someone else, they in turn must reposition themselves in the ways they relate with you.

Moreover, we always teach others how to treat us. This in part explains why a battered woman often escapes one abuser only to connect with another. She inexplicably teaches men how to treat her by the behaviors she accepts and rejects. (Please note I am not advocating the abuse. Abuse is NEVER justified regardless if it is allowed or not). Often she will accept abusive behaviors in the name of "love". Essentially, she is afraid of letting him go.

You cannot be afraid of losing people. If you are going to be an effective long-lasting and loving leader you'll need to love tight, but hold loose. This was a lesson that took me many years to learn.

LOVE TIGHT BUT HOLD LOOSE

During the first six years of my pastorate, I would be devastated whenever anyone would leave our church. "What could I have done differently", I'd always ponder. Sometimes I'd try to convince the departing person that they should stay. That was one of the biggest mistakes I could have ever made.

Whenever you have to convince someone to stay once, you'll have to do it continually. You see, I was reducing my value in the other person's life and training them to treat me and our church like their leftovers. Finally, after years of disappointment, disillusionment, and discouragement a simple truth radically changed me.

Support people in the decisions they make. I know you are thinking, "Is that it?" Yes, but don't overlook the power therein.

First, when you support people in the decision they make, it frees you from the responsibility of their choice. It puts it back on them. They own their decisions for better or for worse.

Secondly, you cannot be accused of manipulation or control.

Thirdly, you proactively determine your response prior to their decision. This prevents you from ever becoming the emotional victim of someone else's choices.

You can end half your troubles immediately by no longer permitting people to tell you what you want.

~ Vernon Howard

I'm glad to say that I am free today. When people determine their "season is up" or "over" or "out" or whatever it may be, I simply give them my blessing. "You don't encourage them to stay, even when you know it's in their best interest?" I hardly ever do, very rarely, almost never. I simply keep moving with the movers.

I've *learned* to love tight, but hold loose. After all, none of the people in our church actually belong to me anyway. None of my clients belong to me either. They *all* belong to God. Staying aware of this reduces my

...love tight, but hold loose.

stress and allows me to focus on my current rather than past assignments. Remember, this calm resolve is the result of my changing not others. Yet inevitably I change how others relate to me.

Ironically, countless people who felt their season was up came back a season or so later. I'm glad to say, they felt the love and acceptance to return. I've been in church nearly all my life and have never seen anything like it. This is the power of supporting people in their decisions. Just like the prodigal son's father, effective leaders know who they are despite who stays, leaves, or even returns. They spend minimum time trying to change others and much of their time changing themselves.

CHANGING SPACES

You may be wondering, "How do I change myself in ways that change how others relate with me?" That's a great question. I'm glad you asked it! Some possible ways to informally increase or reduce the spatial distance between yourself and others include:

Increase Space (farther/more distant)

- Reduce the amount of personal information you share.

- Schedule specific time with a start and ending time.

- Make appointments for meetings rather than engaging in unplanned dialogue.

Reduce Space (closer/more intimate)

- Share small amounts of your heart.

- Increase how much you share as the person shows the ability to protect your heart, remain confidential, and love you more than your formal role.

- Engage in a mutually enjoyable activity together (golf, watching a game, shopping, dining out, etc.).

- Affirm the individual. Speak into the individual's life Tell him about the positive things you see in him.

- Delegate a task or empower the individual to make a decision that reflects your trust for her. You could start on an organizational level and where appropriate move to an individual level. Start small and increase over time based on how they value what you give.

BACK TO PERCEPTION MUSCLES

The second reason I used the term *perception muscle* is that each of us has a level of perception we operate in. Some people are clearly more perceptive than others. They are naturally more intuitive. You know them. Often they say, "I had a feeling that was going to happen". Some just have a gut sense that something is wrong when no one else sees it. Others see visions, have dreams, or a spiritual gift that helps

> **...when two people walk together something unspoken happens. Either one person speeds up or the other slows down... one person adjusts to the other person's pace.**

them make sense of their current reality and future challenges Regardless of which end of the intuition spectrum you find yourself on, like a muscle that is regularly exercised, you can become more perceptive. Until then, keep people around you that see what you don't.

WALK WITH ME?

Choosing who walks with you, the spaces they fill, and the length of time they stay is by far one of the most critical aspects of your leadership assignment. It's been noted that when two people walk together something unspoken happens. Either one person speeds up or the other slows down so the two can walk together. Regardless, one person adjusts to the other person's pace.

My question to you is:

- Whose pace have you adjusted to?
- Who should be adjusting to your pace?
- Are you on track with where you should be now?

- Who have you allowed to slow you down?

Are you leading, but have someone else who's walking too fast? Perhaps they always say you must do this, make that change, or start this endeavor *right now*. While you know these are things you could or even should do, they always seem to move faster than you. It could be a blessing. Perhaps, God is using them to keep your pace up and on point. Conversely, they may be influencing you to move too quickly. Regardless, choosing who walks close with you ultimately influences nearly everything in your leadership and life journey.

Jesus was very intentional about who he chose, the space each disciple had in his life, and the length of their relationship. As a result, 2,000 years later his organization, the Church, has achieved results that Fortune 500 companies can only hope to achieve today. His church went global two centuries ago, has over 2 billion members to date, crosses all barriers (cultural, gender, ethnic, class, generational, language) and has outlasted governments, currencies, every war, horrific persecution, and even internal scandals.

Like Jesus, those that walk with you determine:

- Your long-term success.

- Your perception and credibility in other's eyes.

- If conflict is healthy or destructive in your life.

- The quantity and quality of results you realize.

- Your future success!

Surround yourself with people who sharpen you, challenge you to be your best, and love you enough to tell you the truth, even when it hurts.

LIVING INTO YOUR GREATNESS

Additionally, you need people in your life who challenge you to *live out* your greatness. The Bible declares these types of relationships are mutually beneficial. It says "as iron sharpens iron so people can improve each other " (Proverbs 27:17 New Century Version).

Can I ask you some very personal questions?

- Who in your life regularly encourages you to be better than the day before?

- Who knows you so well that you can't fool them?

- Can you identify at least three people who lift your spirit when they enter the room?

- Who can celebrate your greatness and yet keep you keenly aware of your humanity?

- Who constantly spurs you on to godliness and good works?

- Who loves you enough to tell you it's late go home to your spouse?

You see, every great leader needs supportive relationships in his or her life. You are that great leader; however, you will never live into your greatness without other people. Let me say that again. You will never live into your greatness without other people in your life. In fact, without authentic accountability relationships you will at best be mediocre and at worst be dangerous.

> ...you will never live into your greatness without other people.

Personal relationships are the fertile soil from which all advancement...all success... all achievement in real life grows.

~ Ben Stein

Perhaps you've seen the movie *Spiderman.* In the movie, Uncle Ben told Peter Parker who doubles as Spiderman a relevant truth. Uncle Ben said, "With great power comes great responsibility". As a leader, you have great power and influence over others. With increasing influence comes even greater responsibility. In fact, despite how great an orator, teacher, exhorter, shepherd, accountant, singer, administrator you are, as a leader, your greatest ability is responsibility. This is an ability that all great and long-lasting leaders welcome.

...as a leader, your greatest ability is responsibility.

In case you missed the movie *Spiderman,* which my kids made sure that I saw several times, you may be more familiar with Jesus' words on the same subject. He said, "to whom much is given much is required". Essentially, leaders will have to answer for more because they steward more. Leaders steward more financial resources, talents, gifts, and opportunities. It's foolish to live an unaccountable lifestyle now knowing one day you will give final account to God. It makes sense to prepare for that day now by intentionally building accountability relationships into your life.

...if you are the smartest person in the room you are in the wrong room!

LEVERAGE YOUR WEAKNESSES

Start by observing the people around you. What strengths do they have that you don't? Invite them into the room. Bring them to the table. Leverage your weaknesses with other people's strengths. By doing this, you add value to them, yourself, and your team or organization.

Remember, it's okay to acknowledge other people's strengths around you, even if you are the senior leader in an organization. Being the senior leader doesn't mean that you know it all. The most effective leaders intentionally choose people who are smarter than they are in a particular area or industry. This is true from Fortune 500 companies to the president's cabinet. In fact, if you are the smartest person in the room you are in the wrong room!

Insecure leaders believe they *know it all* and can't learn from others. Secure leaders realize they can learn something from everyone, even if it is what not to do! It has been said, that some people learn from other people's mistakes and the rest have to be the other people. Life is too short for you to make all the mistakes

...some people learn from other people's mistakes and the rest have to be the other people.

yourself! Open up. Learn from others. Watch what works and reject what does not. Most importantly build the mutually beneficial and supportive relationships into your life that you'll need to become all you could be.

I recognize I have not said anything new here. You already know you need these things. The question remains though, "Are you doing them?" I do not mean on paper, in name, or in theory only. Are you doing this for real? Have you made relationships priority in your life or are you off to completing your *next* endeavor?

ARE YOU TASK OR RELATIONSHIP ORIENTATED?

Most leaders, particularly visionary leaders, tend to be "task-orientated" rather than "relationship-orientated". This is what helps them get things done. Neither task-orientation nor relationship-orientation is better than the other. In fact, you have both in you. You were created by God to live in community with others (relationship-orientation) and to use the gifts He's given you to get things done (task-orientation).

Leadership always involves other people.

It's just that you naturally lean towards one orientation more than the other. Either you are more comfortable working with people or handling tasks. Whichever you are most comfortable doing is your default mode. Like your computer settings, it is what you naturally resort to unless you are challenged otherwise. This means over time you operated more in one mode, task or relationships, than the other. This made you stronger in that area.

Generally task-orientated leaders see a vision, have a dream, make a to-do list, and move to get it accomplished. Often they do so with great success, at least initially. You see, every vision, each task, and all major accomplishments require other's efforts to be realized. While task orientated leaders win in the short term, as their vision is fulfilled, often they lose in the long-term. This happens because often they underestimate the *sustaining relationships* around them that have made them successful.

...each relationship in your life is either increasing in value or decreasing in value depending on how much you invest into it.

Resultantly, over time people feel a gambit of emotions from overlooked and insignificant to manipulated and used. One by one or even in groups they begin to withhold or remove their time, talents, and treasure as they further disconnect from the vision. Ultimately, the supportive ground the leader stands on is removed as the needed relationships unravel.

There is something to be said of leadership and relationships. While there are over five hundred differing definitions of the word leadership, one thing can be agreed upon—leadership always involves other people. Therefore, it is a relationship of some

If you are task-orientated you'll need to *intentionally* make relationships a priority in your life.

type. It could be a relationship with a group of constituents, a congregation, an employee, or even a student or child. Nevertheless, it is always a relationship of some sorts.

ADDING VALUE TO YOUR RELATIONSHIPS

All relationships are fluid, they change over time. Therefore, each relationship in your life is either increasing in value or decreasing in value depending on how much you invest into it. This is true with your spouse, children, friends, peers, employees, and even God your father. As a leader, you need to increase you relational equity. If not you may find, like many American homeowners did when the housing bubble busted, your relationships no longer appraise for what they did when you both first bought into them.

You can increase your relational equity by intentionally investing into it your relationships. Doing so, ultimately means investing into the individual person(s) you are connected to. This is a proactive move towards damage control. Certainly it is a worthwhile investment of your effort and time.

If you are task-orientated you'll need to *intentionally* make relationships a priority in your life. To begin or renew your commitment to this ask yourself a few questions:

- What would my relationship to_____ look like if it were top priority in my life? Describe it.

- Who needs to know just how much I value their person (more than their position or work) in my life?

- Who do I request more out of than I deposit into? How can I make deposits into him/her that add value to him/her?

- Who are the 20% of people in my life that contribute to 80% of my fulfillment and personal effectiveness?

- What changes do I need to make to my checkbook and calendar to reflect my commitment and priority to my relationships?

I cannot underscore enough the importance of this commitment. As a Christian, God says the first and most important commandment is to love Him with all your heart, soul, mind, and strength and the second is equally important. Love your neighbor as yourself. The Great Commandment reveals the great priority God puts on relationships. As a leader, your responsibility to do the same only increases not decreases.

This may overwhelm you at first. However, don't overburden yourself with thoughts of how challenging this is for you. As a task orientated person I certainly understand. So here's what I say, begin where you are.

- Crawl until you can walk.

- Take small steps and commit to the process of developing your relationships.

- If you notice your relationship(s) is coasting along, it is because it is probably going downhill!

Chapter 4

- Remain aware of your tendency to put work or things before people.

- Remember the most important things in life are not things, they are relationships.

James 3:18, in *The Message* paraphrase says, "You can develop a healthy, robust community that lives right with God and enjoy its results *only* if you do the hard work of getting along with each other, treating each other with dignity and honor." Yes, people and relationships are hard work but everything worth anything requires work and a personal investment.

Besides, every resource you've ever received has always come through relationships. Think about that. It is true from breast milk to business loans. Never underestimate the importance of relationships in your life. I guarantee your next blessing will come through a person or a relationship of some sorts.

4

DAMAGE CONTROL:
The Leader and His Relationships

Dr. Samuel R. Chand

People are right. I am living a charmed life. My wonderful life is all built on one word—Relationships. People joke that I know more people than there are people. My friend John Maxwell says that when we get to heaven..."Sam will be standing next to Jesus introducing Him to everyone". It's almost true!

In the supernatural it is divine favor—the God factor.

In the natural it is human favor—relationships.

> **...your vision fulfillment is totally dependent on who's holding your ladder.**

Charles Tremendous Jones once said that five years from now you'll be the same person except for the books you read and people with whom you associate.

In my book, *Who's Holding Your Ladder?* I explain that your ascent up your visionary ladder is not dependent on your vision (the ladder) or your ladder climbing skills—your vision fulfillment is totally dependent on who's holding your ladder.

In leadership the most critical decision you will make is selecting your leaders—relationships.

Whenever I am looking for ladder holders who can walk in relationship with me in my vision walk I look for five qualities:

1. STRONG—they can handle instruction and correction without crumbling.

2. ATTENTIVE—they can learn quickly and don't need repetitious training.

3. FAITHFUL—they have faith in their visionary leader.

4. FIRM—they are not blown about by manipulative people.

5. LOYAL—agreement with me doesn't make one loyal and disagreement with me doesn't make one disloyal. My definition of loyalty is that you can disagree with my head but not my heart. You can disagree with how I do things, but not why I do them. You can disagree with my methods, but not my motivations.

> **The voices in your ear—past and present will determine your life's direction.**

Show me the caller ID on your phone and I will tell you where your life is right now and where you are headed.

The voices in your ear—past and present will determine your life's direction.

Remember when dad and mom would not let you play with certain kids *("They're bad for you...")* or warned you about your relationships as a young adult *("They're bad for you...")*? They did it for a purpose. They knew that more than anything else your relationships will define you.

However, when we get older (not necessarily wiser) we don't have our parents to tell us *"They're bad for you..."* and so we wander into relationships at our peril. Who in your life has permission to say to you, *"They're bad for you."?*

While the old adage *birds of a feather flock together* is true so is its corollary. We are known not just by the company we keep, but also by the people (birds) we stay away from.

> **None of us have "come" here. All of us have been "brought" here.**

While my first meeting with people is a convergence of divine coincidences my next connection with them (if there is to be one) is intentional.

Reflect on your primary relationships—they're all intentional.

Low level relationships are accidental. Life-long and high level relationships are intentional.

It must also be noted that relationships are fragile and need to be handled with great care. Good relationships are a product of nurturing.

You are where you are in life because of relationships. None of us have "come" here. All of us have been "brought" here.

If you see a turtle sitting on top of a fence-post you know one thing—the turtle did not get there by itself!

So my dear brother turtles and sister turtlettes, don't forget who brought you here. Whenever someone says, "I'm a self made man." I feel like responding with, "Didn't make much of yourself, did you?"

Relationships are enhanced when we share life and its credits with those who brought us here.

Choose your primary relationships carefully because they will define your future as well as your legacy.

5

DISASTER RECOVERY:
Mission Still Possible!

Dr. Don Brawley III

Expect the best. Prepare for the worst.

Capitalize on what comes.

~ Zig Ziglar

DISASTER PLANNING GUIDE

I once took a speech class where each student was required to write and deliver a persuasive speech. I heard a story I'll never forget. While I can't remember my speech, now twenty years later, I still remember one young lady's speech.

Her speech was entitled, "Don't Go to Mexico!" It detailed, from start to finish, her traumatic experiences there. She intended on preventing others from experiencing the harrowing circumstances she endured. Her unbelievable story was told something like this.

"Don't go to Mexico. I went and as a result I just finished one year of therapy. (She said this with a smile and yet silent tears streaming down her face). A few friends and I saved and prepared for our trip to Mexico. We didn't make a lot of money, but we put our pennies together and were determined to have a great trip and enjoy the beach in Mexico.

We arrived early for our flight out of JFK airport in New York City. With great anticipation we boarded our plane for the trip of a lifetime. It was definitely a trip I'll never forget. After we boarded our plane the pilot proceeded towards the runway. As we waited for clearance we smelled smoke. Not only did we smell smoke, but we saw it too. After we debarked, we found out that the engine was on fire. Although we were thankful that the malfunction occurred while we were on the ground we had to wait all day to catch another plane to Mexico. I didn't let that stop me from having a good time. I said, 'It's okay, it's just part of the trip'.

> **Show me someone who hasn't endured a setback and I'll show you someone who has not began a journey.**

We finally flew on another flight and landed in Mexico. Although we prepaid our ground transportation we arrived so late that the company was closed for the night. So, my friends and I hired a taxi driver to take us to our hotel which was less than five minutes drive from the airport. Our driver didn't speak English and charged us in Pesos not dollars. It wasn't until the next morning that we discovered he charged us the equivalent of fifty US dollars to take us around the corner. That didn't matter. You know why? It was just part of the trip.

> **...setbacks always cost. The sooner you rebound the less you pay.**

When we arrived at our hotel we were overwhelmed, not with joy, but by all the roaches that filled our room. On top of that, the hotel didn't look anything like the picture we saw. We asked for another room and were told the hotel was at capacity. We slept with one eye open in horror from the roach infestation around us. Somehow we endured the night and I told the other girls, 'It's just part of the trip.'

Eventually we found another hotel, directly on the beach, and we successfully negotiated a refund from our first hotel. Soon after settling in, my stomach became very unsettled. Before I knew it, I began making several quick dashes to the toilet.

The next day my friends took me to the clinic. The doctor told me I had dysentery and prescribed medication to treat it. Apparently, I got it from drinking the water there. I took the medicine and broke out with red bumps all over my body. It turns out I was **...a fast paced environment often means your plans are outdated before they are totally implemented.** allergic to the medication. I kept telling myself that everything was okay. It was simply just part of the trip.

After a couple days I began to feel better. I wanted to get out and enjoy my trip. Part of my reason for going to Mexico was to skydive.

I had long dreamed of skydiving and thought now is my chance. I patiently waited my turn until something went horrifically wrong. The man just in front of me died of a heart attack right before my eyes. That wasn't part of the trip and I knew it! Of course my plans for skydiving were quickly cancelled and I opted for something safe like sunbathing on the beach.

Looking back, I don't know why I expected sunbathing would be smooth and easy. Nothing else to this point had been. Nevertheless, I laid out on the beach and actually enjoyed myself. As the sun began setting **...plan in pencil.** I collected my belongings and walked along the boardwalk towards the hotel.

At this point, I stopped to get ice cream. A man who looked like Elvis came out of nowhere and stepped on my toe with

> **Being adaptable means you may bend, but you won't break.**

his thick heeled shoes! I screamed and stood in disbelief. Before I knew it, I was back at the clinic again only to find I had a broken toe! I went home with horrific memories and vowed I'd never return to Mexico."

By the time the young lady finished telling her story our entire class applauded. We were all proud of her courage. Despite her ordeal and subsequent counseling she made it through her storm. While most of what she'd experienced no one could have specifically prepared for, this young lady personified two essential qualities to disaster recovery and weathering any storm: resiliency and adaptability.

BE RESILIENT...BE ADAPTABLE...BE READY!

Resiliency is the ability to recover quickly from setbacks. Storms can set you back. Disasters can set you back. People can set you back. The economic or social environment can set you back. Things in and out of your control can set you back. You can even set yourself back!

Setbacks are a part of life's journey. In fact, set backs are just part of the trip! Show me someone who hasn't endured a setback and I'll show you someone who has not began a journey. It's not a matter of if you will have any setbacks, but rather how you will respond to them when they occur. The more resilient you are the quicker you'll recover and the less it will cost you.

All setbacks cost something. When a builder is setback it cost him money and perhaps manpower. When a commuter is setback it cost her time away from her family and extra gas.

When a quarterback is setback it could cost him a first down or ultimately the game. When a politician is setback it could cost him an election or reelection. Regardless of who you are or what you do, setbacks always cost. The sooner you rebound the less you pay.

The second quality you'll need is adaptability. Adaptability is the ability to change easily. In other words you can adjust easily to a different environment or new conditions. Since change is the order of the day, adaptability is paramount for both leaders and their organizations.

Often changing conditions will require you to rethink how you do what you do. Sometimes this means rethinking your plan. While there is great value in strategic planning a fast paced environment often means your plans are outdated before they are totally implemented.

Does this mean you shouldn't plan? Absolutely not! It means you should plan in pencil. Your plan and your people should be capable of changing to suit different circumstances. Remember your plan is a living document.

Like a pilot you'll need to remain adaptable and flexible so you can make changes to your flight plan when necessary. An old proverb says, "Blessed are the flexible for they shall not be bent out of shape". Being adaptable means you may bend, but you won't break.

Quick and constant change requires both resiliency and adaptability. The extent you build these ingredients into your life and your organization determines the extent you'll rebound from and survive unexpected disasters.

DID YOU KNOW...?

- Almost 50% of small to medium sized companies without a disaster recovery plan go out of business after a disaster? [1]

- Fires permanently close 44% of the business affected.

- In the 1993 World Trade Center bombing, 150 of 350 businesses affected failed to survive the event.[2]

- Conversely, the firms affected by the September 11th attacks with well-developed and tested Business Continuity Planning Manuals were back in business within days.[3]

Whatever could go wrong, may go wrong. You can't go wrong by preparing for the worst and praying for the best!

~ Murphy's Law revised

However, not all disasters are completely unexpected. Many can be avoided with just a little planning. Others can't be avoided, but their affects can be significantly reduced. Both require planning, coordination, and communication.

Inside the cover of this book is a code. Visit www.donbrawley. com to access your *Weathering the Storm: Leading in Uncertain Times* disaster recovery template.

N OTES
1. Stohr, Edward A. Business Continuity in the Pharmaceutical Industry. Hoboken: Howe School of Technology Management, 2004.
2. Continuity of operations planning. U.S. Department of Homeland Security. Retrieved July 6, 2006.
3. Ibid.

5

DISASTER RECOVERY:
Mission Still Possible!

Dr. Samuel R. Chand

Recovering from disaster is hard work. A disaster creates its own history. It makes an indelible impression that affects the future.

I fly a lot. I mean a lot. I take approximately 200 flights a year. I get some of my best stories in the airport. If someone's flight is delayed they will exclaim out loud, "I will never ever fly _____ airlines again." These are occasional travelers for whom a delayed flight is disastrous and defining.

> **A disaster creates its own history.**

My family and I were in India in November 2008 when the Mumbai massacre took place. In fact we were in the very same hotel just two days prior to that. On the night of that tragic disaster when terrorists killed scores of people all over Mumbai at random, we were all sleeping hundreds of miles away in Lucknow, my home town. Our phone rang. It was our pastor in the US wondering if we were all right. We told him yes and then he asked us have you watched the news? Out came our laptops and we saw the disaster unfold. That disaster changed our plans immediately. For a couple days I kept my family indoors not wanting to give some copy cat the temptation to do anything stupid. Instead of flying back through Mumbai, we came through Paris (that was the expensive part—shopping in Paris is not cheap!). So what happens on our next trip? Will we go to Mumbai? Will we go back to that hotel? For me the answer is yes, but can certainly be dif- ferent for many other people.

Disasters, natural or manmade, can become defining moments.

Disasters, natural or manmade, can become defining moments.

Disasters define us more than when all is well. No one remembers a routine wedding, but a disastrous one—who can forget?

Don't make long term decisions based on disastrous events.

So, how do we recover from disasters?

1. Understand that this was an isolated incident and not necessarily the rule.

2. Don't make long term decisions based on disastrous events.

3. Use disasters to learn from them. I travel extensively— domestically as well as internationally but never check my luggage. It's always carry on. I learned from my "lost-luggage disaster " that I can pack less, but have it with me.

Relax. Inhale. Exhale. You'll be okay.

4. Be flexible. Disaster recovery is harder for those who cannot bend with the situation.

5. Adapt quickly. You can analyze later and make strong pronouncements and judgments at another time. But in the midst of disaster recovery, adapt.

Live another day and you will come across disaster—yours or someone else's. Relax. Inhale. Exhale. You'll be okay.

6

FINDING COURAGE
FACING CHANGE

Dr. Don Brawley III

*God, grant me the serenity to accept
the things I cannot change,
Courage to change the things I can,
And wisdom to know the difference.*

~ Reinhold Niebuhr

It was a day planned months in advance, packed with fun and adventure. We'd ride a few hours from Long Island to upstate New York and enjoy the day at Rye Beach Play Land Amusement Park. Of course, for a high school aged student to really have fun, food and friends were part of the excitement. I couldn't wait till that day finally came.

We all met up at the church early that Saturday morning. One of my friends, who'd just graduated college and recently purchased a brand new Buick Regal, asked a few of us if we wanted to ride in his new car. Hmm, ride in a new car with your closest friends or find a seat on the church's cheese bus? Well that was a no brainer! So with Michael we went.

Michael had never driven to this particular park or that far for that matter. Keep in mind this was a few decades before the luxury of GPS became commonplace. We were a little concerned about that but he assured us it would be no problem. He'd already talked with the bus driver and would simply follow her lead to the park. So we got in his car, turned up the music, let the windows down and followed the bus down the Long Island Expressway.

Everything was going just great... well, that is until it wasn't anymore. Michael, enjoying the drive, got a little ahead of himself and the bus for that matter. To be clearer, he decided to shift from behind the bus to the left side of the bus. Little did he know that just as he moved left the bus exited right towards the Whitestone Bridge. In a matter of moments, we were headed straight for Manhattan while the rest of our group was headed upstate New York towards the park.

I can still picture my other friends on the bus pointing their fingers at our car as they laughed and the distance grew wider between our car and their bus. In the moment I could see the humor in it all. After all, who would've known he'd go to the left of the bus at the precise moment the bus would exit right? However, that got old real quick. After stopping multiple times and getting conflicting directions to the park, it was no longer funny, not at all.

Well we eventually made it to the amusement park; however, quite unamused! It was well after 4pm, several hours later. Our group had already ridden the rides and had just gathered to have food together before loading up and heading home. So those of us who rode in Michael's car never got to ride any of the rides in the park. Who knew the most thrilling ride of the day would turn out to be the car ride there!

Nonetheless, looking back three decades (I'm finally over it now, well at least I'd like believe that I am), what that day lacked in amusement and adventure it more than made up for in lessons.

---
we don't lose people when we're traveling straight; we lose them in the turns.

The biggest of these is that we don't lose people when we're traveling straight; we lose them in the turns. We lose people who follow us in the transitions.

TRANSITIONS

Those of us who were in the car were very frustrated that Michael decided to drive next to the bus he was supposed to follow. After all, he knew before leaving that he didn't know where he was going. So why in the world would he move from behind the bus driver who knew how to get us to our destination? Seeing Michael's shortfall was fairly obvious. But seeing the larger leadership issue wasn't initially as apparent. Similarly, for most leaders this is where they lose people they're called to lead.

The bus driver had made this trip several times before. She could get to that park and back home again in her sleep. She had a CDL driver's license and was a highly experienced driver. She also knew our car was following the bus she drove. Finally, she knew up ahead she needed to make the impending turn. However, she didn't signal to Michael that she would be going right. If she did, he would've remained behind her. Her signal would've given him the time he needed to follow her lead and make the upcoming lane change in the highway.

That's what leaders do. They give signals. They give time for people to adjust and change directions. They help their people transition. No matter what road you're leading your people on now; eventually you'll have to make a change to get to your destination. Despite modern day GPS applications, the leader will always be the most vital voice of both change and transition to the people who follow.

GPS

No matter which GPS system you use, each one does the same basic functions. First, it locates where you currently are. Second, it maps out where you're going. Third, it tells you when to turn and in what direction. Lastly, perhaps the most overlooked yet vital function is it tells you ahead of time what adjustments you need to make long before your next turn.

all too often leaders tell their people the turn but don't give them time to make the adjustments.

"In two miles exit to your left 231b, towards Atlanta." A few moments later, your GPS would then say something like, "in one mile exit left 231b towards Atlanta". All along your GPS is giving you time to get in the correct lane and make adjustments so you don't miss your turn. Unfortunately, all too often leaders tell their people the turn but don't give them time to make the adjustments. They don't give them time to transition.

TRANSITION VERSUS CHANGE

So how exactly is transition different from change? Simply put, change is an event. It's the actual turn. However, transition has to do with how the turn (change) affects people. Specifically, transition includes how people internally process the effects of change in three ways: emotionally, psychologically, and relationally. How do the people who are following my bus emotionally internalize our next turn? How do they mentally process the change in highways we're driving on? How will the changes we're making affect the relationships they have? These questions aren't about the actual change; instead, they are about the transitions change brings.

You see, change can happen in a moment but transitions always take time. That's where the bus driver failed us on our

trip. She was leading us. We were following her. She knew
the way yet she made a quick change without giving Michael a chance to transition with her. As a result, we lost valuable time and

> **change can happen in a moment but transitions always take time.**

ultimately didn't have a great experience that day. Moreover, we didn't get to connect with the rest of our group who rode the bus that day either. It affected our relationships; at least for that day. Disconnect is what happens when a change is made without considering the transitional needs of everyone on the journey.

> **Disconnect is what happens when a change is made without considering the transitional needs of everyone on the journey.**

Again, change happens in a moment but transitions take time.

BACK TO THE FUTURE

In Joshua 1:2, God says something that is very interesting. He tells Joshua, *Moses my servant is dead. Now therefore, arise go over this Jordan, you and all this people to the land which I am giving to them—even to the children of Israel.*[1] Many translations begin verse 1 with the English word "Now" which in Hebrew is actually "and". I find that to be an interesting way to start a new book… "And". However, a closer study shows that the book of Joshua isn't only canonized directly after Deuteronomy but its storyline picks up where Deuteronomy ends.

Chapter thirty-four gives us a brief overview of Moses' life and the general vicinity of where he was buried. Deuteronomy ends with all of Israel mourning Moses' death. So why would God pick up in Joshua's book by announcing, "Moses my servant is dead?" After all, Joshua was Moses assistant pastor, if you will, and like all of Israel had already mourned his death for thirty days. Surely Joshua knew Moses was dead!

However, there is a big difference between knowing something and accepting it. Sure Joshua knew Moses was dead; however, he hadn't accepted it yet. Notice, Joshua couldn't arise and go over "this Jordan", until he first accepted Moses' death. Similarly, people can't get beyond what they haven't gotten over. The patriarch's death was the change, an event; however, accepting it was a huge part of his successor's transition.

> **there is a big difference between knowing something and accepting it.**

> **people can't get beyond what they haven't gotten over.**

God gives us an exemplary leadership lesson. Despite Joshua knowing of Moses' death, mourning him and the calendar advancing we see God rewind the tape and visit Joshua back at Moses' death. That's because that's where Joshua got stuck. You see, God doesn't meet you where you think you are; He meets you where you actually are. Although Joshua had mourned Moses at least 30 days prior he was still at least thirty days behind. So instead of God ignoring that, He met Joshua at the place where he got stuck. That's what leaders do.

You can't ask people who follow your lead to arise towards your vision and cross the next challenge before them until you first deal with the last transition behind them. You must go backwards to the place where they were last stuck. Not only that but sometimes even as the leader

> **You must go backwards to the place where they were last stuck.**

you too must go back to where you last got stuck when things changed. In these fast-paced changing times, more often than ever before, leaders face unanticipated changes and can more easily get stuck themselves.

I've never been in jail literally but I certainly have gone fugitively more times than I care to remember. Specifically, I've been in jail while playing the board game Monopoly®. It's nothing like wanting to get ahead, move around the board, and acquire properties only to watch everyone else pass you by while you're stuck in jail. Perhaps this is a metaphor for how people feel when we lead forward while they're left behind still processing the fallout of our last change. It's easy for them to feel like they've lost their turn over and over again.

DEALING WITH TRANSITION

As a visionary, you're probably ready to roll the dice and make your move. However, your team, staff, leaders, and volunteers may still be mourning the last change, the last move, or perhaps their last lost turn. Unfortunately, when you cast fresh vision you may face a lack luster commitment to moving towards it. You're thinking new gains but they're feeling old losses. Sometimes the reason for these feelings are unbeknown to them but more often than not it can be traced backwards to a previous roll of the die; a change that someone hadn't fully transitioned through.

All change involves loss. Let me say that again. All change involves loss. That includes changes that seem good. Noted psychologist Steven Grosz says life is a series of changes that always include loss. When a baby gains solid food she loses her mother's breast. When she goes to school she loses the intimacy of home care. When a young man marries though he gains a wife he loses the family dynamics and home of his youth. Each of these changes is good; yet, each inherently involves a loss of some sort.

So what's a leader to do? Well, I'm sure you don't want to hold people's hands through each and every change. Need I say, that'd be unhealthy for both parties anyway! Instead of holding their hands, hold their hearts; after all, it's been said that leadership is an affair of the heart. Let me explain.

Leadership, like any other interpersonal dynamic, is a relationship. In order for a relationship to remain healthy and productive, both parties must keep their finger on the pulse, or the heart of it. As the leader, your role is to discover where your people are, even when they can't articulate it themselves, so that you can move them to the place where they could be. That's why God had to say to Joshua, "Moses my servant is dead." God took the lead in articulating where Joshua was stuck and then showed him where he could go after he was unstuck.

KNOWING VERSUS ACCEPTING

As I stated earlier, there's a huge difference between knowing something and accepting it. Just because a person knows something doesn't mean they've accepted it. For example, think about how many alcoholics know they have a drinking problem but haven't truly accepted it yet. Whenever people don't accept it, whatever the "it" may be, they will not be able to arise into the new opportunities opened by the change they resist.

For many years as a new pastor, stuck was my address. For the first seven years of our ministry, whenever anyone left our church of course I knew they'd left but I struggled accepting it. Their leaving was the change but I got stuck in the transition. Looking back I can clearly see the cycle because my thoughts, like a broken record, replayed the same way each time. First, when the news came that John Smith and his family were leaving it was the dreaded feeling inside like the bottom dropped out of my soul. But then came the series of questions: what did I do wrong, how could I be better, how could I convince them to stay, etc. Even worst, I prayed with people to stay, gave them "a word" about them staying and indirectly begged people to stay. My behavior bordered on pitiful at best and self-sabotaging at worse.

It would be years later before I'd discover that anyone who leaves isn't essential for your destiny. Moreover, you always devalue yourself whenever you ask someone to stay who chooses to walk out of your life. Yet the issue had so much less to do with them and so much more to do with me. It showed me how I handled change, how I'd get stuck transitioning through the inevitable changes that come in organizational life, particularly the local church.

After years of repeating the same unhealthy behaviors, praying, and asking other pastors how they dealt with people leaving one day I got my "Get Out of Jail Card!" God spoke to my heart so clearly and said, "Don, support *their* decisions". Wait God, what if I know they're supposed to be here? What if they're making a bad decision? It didn't matter. I was to support their decision and let them own their decision just as God had done for me time and time again. That was one of the most liberating moments of my entire life. That was the day I learned to accept what I couldn't change and later, in hindsight, realized I never needed to.

When I think about that freeing moment and how deeply it's impacted my leadership journey and more importantly my life, I stand in utter gratefulness for the lesson, though painful, I learned. You cannot arise until you first accept. Accept the pain. Accept the loss. Accept the betrayal. Accept the season.

> **You cannot arise until you first accept.**

Accept human weakness. Accept it all. For it's in accepting, not knowing, that you access your "Get out of Jail Card" and find new liberty to get back in the game. While it's true change involves loss it brings new opportunities too.

5 STAGES OF GRIEF

As I said earlier, your job as leader is to discover where your people are as it relates to transitioning, so you can move them forward. Since all change involves loss, I thought I'd take a moment to consider the 5 Stages of Grief. If you're already aware of them, I want you to make the connection between them and leadership transitions. If you're unfamiliar with them, no worries, we'll take a look at them now.

The 5 Stages of Grief are: shock & denial, pain & guilt, anger & bargaining, depression & loneliness, and acceptance & hope. Each stage has its unique characteristics. Despite the title 5 Stages of Grief, further studies have emphasized grief doesn't flow in a linear fashion. Instead the thoughts we think and feeling we experience are often more like a sea of emotions with unpredictable tides. Nonetheless, for the context of leadership they provide a suitable framework for how people handle change, how they transition. The better we are at transitioning ourselves and at helping those whom we lead, the more capable we'll be of riding out the exponential increase of change and the storms it can bring.

Stage 1: Shock & Denial

May sound something like…

    a. *I can't believe so and so left our church!*
    b. *What do you mean we're ending Sunday school and starting small groups?*
    c. *I can't believe even though I'm qualified that I wasn't chosen for the position!*

Stage 2: Pain & Guilt

May sound something like…

    a. *How could they leave after all we've done for them?*
    b. *Maybe if I'd supported the Sunday school more we'd still have one.*
    c. *After all these years that I've served faithfully here, I'm so hurt that they could just overlook me like that.*

Stage 3: Anger & Bargaining

May sound something like…

    a. Maybe if I asked them to be on the new building committee they will stay

    b. I'm so angry. My late grandmother started our Sunday school ministry. Who are they to end it?

    c. Maybe if I talk directly to the pastor he will see that I get that position.

Stage 4: Depression & Loneliness

May sound something like…

    a. Man I'm in this thing all alone. People say one thing then do another. I can't count on anybody but God.

    b. Seems like everyone is so excited about the new small groups ministry except for me. I feel so sad every time I think about how Sunday school used to be.

    c. Well everyone is excited that Bob got the position. Good for him but what about me?

Stage 5: Acceptance & Hope

May sound something like…

    a. It's been a few months since the Jones' left. Things are still happening. I met a new brother. He's so eager to serve; he's passionate about our vision.

    b. I went with my husband to a couples' small group last night. It was the first time we've studied the bible together with other couples.

    c. Bob is a great person to work alongside. Since I don't have the extra responsibilities of that position I have more time to practice with the band.

Hopefully reading these fictitious examples helps you see where you are and or where the people who follow you may be stuck. Please don't feel the need to "diagnose" everyone in your organization. The thought of that alone would make me sick!

Instead, if you see individuals struggling through a current transition or are stuck in a previous one give the gift of understanding and support. If you happen to be the one who is stuck find someone who can give you that same gift of understanding and support. I consult with pastors all the time who feel alone in the trenches and am grateful that God would use the pain of ministry I've endured to strengthen, encourage, and move other pastors forward. Though at the time I didn't see those painful experiences as a blessing, today I realize they were a gift to me that I just could never keep to myself.

As a leader, here are a few gifts you can give your people while transitioning:

1. An understanding ear. Once you know where someone is you can better understand him or her. You're not called to change them but as a leader you can challenge them.

   You're not called to change them but as a leader you can challenge them.

   Like God did with Joshua, help others see where they actually are and show them that you genuinely care about them and their feelings.

2. Time. People process loss, grief, and change at different speeds. Allow time for transitioning by being a GPS that announces a change is coming up the road long before it does. Then give people the time they need to process it and position themselves so they make the turn when it comes. Just like driving, whenever you make a turn it's only complete afterwards when the wheel is straightened. Simply put, transition requires time before the turn, in the turn, and after the turn. Allow people time to turn at their own pace so they avoid running off the road. Remember change isn't a one speed fits all! We'll talk a little more about this later.

3. Communication. People are always down on what they're not up on. The best way to help your people transition through change is by establishing regular communication intervals and channels. Use

---
People are always down on what they're not up on.

---

communication to give information and to receive feedback. Remember communication is always a two-way street.

4. Grace. Often leaders are hardest on themselves. They think I should be over this by now. This shouldn't bother me the way it still does. Exhale. Give yourself grace to transition. As you do so, remember to extend the same to those who follow your lead too.

You may be thinking, okay some of this is easier said than done. If so, well you're right. It's not easy; but it is doable. Leadership is never easy but it certainly can be well worth it.

EMBRACING CHANGE

Since writing the first edition of this book one thing has become increasingly clear. Change is happening at an exponential rate. A few game-changers have fueled the speed and increase of change: smart phones, cloud storage, exponential growth of social media platforms, real time customer feedback ratings, online marketplaces (Airbnb, Amazon), streaming services, new delivery systems, growth of non-contractual commitments (gym, phone services), increase in automation and the youngest of the largest generation in history, The Millennial Generation, are now all adults. These are just some current drivers of rapid change. Each of these drivers affect how we work, socialize, plan, gather, delegate, deliver services and what people expect from us. Essentially, they demand we change.

They demand we change faster and more often than ever before. Don't get me wrong; you don't have to change who you are or your mission. Rather, you must change *how* you do what you do. The people you serve are being trained by these societal changes on what to expect and even more so how they should expect what they get

Organizations that don't adapt will not survive.

and give to your organization. They expect excellent, fast, and engaging service as the norm not the exception. Organizations that don't adapt will not survive. Therefore, they need leaders who are themselves adaptable and willing to change to lead them. You don't have to like change to embrace it. But you do need to accept it before you can benefit from it. While speed is certainly important as it relates to keeping up in a changing world, transition can't be rushed or calendared.

Since everyone moves through transition at different paces it's beneficial to recognize it. Leaders who recognize this can avoid being discouraged or frustrated by those who need more time making a transition. Also, they can better focus their time and energy with those who are ready for the change that fresh vision brings.

According to Roger's Bell Curve individuals accept an innovation or change within a defined adopter group. In simple terms, people adopt a change based on one of five categories they belong to: innovators, early adopters, early majority, late majority and laggards. Essentially, your innovators will either come up with the idea or "get it" as soon as they hear it. Your early adopters will follow right behind your innovators. These two groups are relatively small as is the laggard group. These

leaders should spend the majority of their time and energy with those in the middle who are waiting to be led by them.

three groups together make up less than 40 percent of the people.

Leaders often spend the vast majority of their time with people who will get it quickly and agree with them or never get it and oppose them. Instead, leaders should spend the majority of their time and energy with those in the middle who are waiting to be led by them. Those in the middle, the early majority and late majority are just that, the majority! They're not fighting you they just want to understand you, why "we" need to change, and be allowed time to do so.

I'm going to be blunt here. Stop wasting your time with folks who oppose you, who resist change *just because* and who just don't want to get it. Instead, fire up and release your innovators

change is inevitable but growth is optional.

and early adopters to influence your early majority and late majority. Recognize your laggards may never get it but your early majority followed by your late majority will get it in time. Then adjust your energy and expectations accordingly. Move with the movers. Keep in mind, change is inevitable but growth is optional.

You should expect hyper-change to be your new normal. It will continue coming faster. You will need to master transitions in order to reduce unnecessary storms and lead through the uncertainty change brings. Even when you don't know exactly how things will come together you must communicate what you do know, repeatedly. This gives those who you lead greater clarity about where they are and confidence in where you're leading them.

Joshua didn't know *how* he'd get Israel across the Jordan but he did know they would cross it. He'd seen the land 40 years prior. He walked it. He ate from it. He described it. He had a vision. He didn't have to have all the answers upfront as to how they'd get to it but he had to have courage and strength while transitioning. If you lead with courage, you too can get to your promised land and see your vision realized.

REVIEW AND REFLECT

1. Leaders don't' lose people when traveling straight. They lose them when they make a turn or in the transitions.

   - What were the last 3-5 changes you made?

   - How well did the people affected by the change transition?

   - Who's stuck in the last change? What do they need from you to move forward? (Support, empathy, information, time, clarity, etc.)

2. Change happens in a moment. Transition happens over time.

   - People accept change within an adapter group: innovators, early adopters, early majority, late majority and laggards.

   - The innovators and adopters will "get it" then laggards may never "get it".

   - Focus on the early majority and late majority.

3. ALL leaders, not just senior leaders, are responsible for leading transition within the organization.

   - List the names of those within your sphere of influence.

   - How do they need you to show up so they can make the turn?

4. Leaders are departmental or organizational GPS' that announce a change or a "turn" is coming, giving people ample time to effectively transition.

   - Who should hear about a forthcoming change first? Second and so on?

- What mode of communication should each receive the information? (In person, a private meeting, small group meeting, pulpit announcement, e-blast, social media, etc.)

5. People can't get beyond what they haven't gotten over.

   - Often times going backwards is the only way to bring people forward with you.

   - You may have to go backwards and meet people where they are, not where you thought they should be by now.

   - Help those who are stuck in the past move towards acceptance and to see the benefits before them.

   - Be gracious.

6. Leaders should spend the majority of their efforts on transitions not change.

7. Change is inevitable; but growth is optional.

   - Adaptable leaders will survive and thrive in hyper-change.

   - Adaptable leaders will grow during times of challenge and change.

   - In what ways as a leader are you adapting to change?

   - What growth opportunity do you see for yourself in how you adapt to change?

   - How would those you lead better transition through change as you better adapt to it?

N OTES

1. 1. Stephen, Grosz, (2014). The Examined Life: How we Lose and Find Ourselves
2. New King James Bible. (1972) Bible Gateway- http://www.biblegateway.com/ versions/New-King-Jame.
3. Rogers, Everett M. (1962). *Diffusion of Innovations*, Glencoe: Free Press

6

FINDING COURAGE FACING CHANGE

Dr. Samuel R. Chand

Life is pleasant. Death is peaceful.
It's the transition that's troublesome.

~ Isaac Asimov, Novelist and Scholar

Teisha had been in charge of the accounting department at her company for over seven years and had been successful. Recently her boss Matt, asked if she would consider moving to the marketing department. He needed a seasoned manager to handle things in that area. Always interested in numbers, the new challenges of marketing analysis interested her. She agreed to make the move. On Monday, Matt announced the change; Teisha packed up her stuff and moved to an office on the seventh floor near the marketing team. The change was easy, but the transition was not.

As soon as Matt announced Teisha's change, the gossiping

started. Was an accountant qualified to lead marketing? Who would be the next accounting manager? Was Teisha responsible for the previous marketing manager's firing? John had worked in marketing for five years; why wasn't he picked to be the marketing manager? Didn't Matt know people in the marketing department didn't like Teisha because she always demanded receipts for their reimbursements? And so it went.

CHANGE VS. TRANSITION

Change is the result of a decision. It is an external event. Moving Teisha from accounting to marketing is a change. It was announced, she moved her office, it is done.

Transition, on the other hand, is the emotional, relational, financial, and psychological processing of change. Transitions are internal. In this example, the

Transitions are internal.

transition included fears about the new leadership, affinities with the old marketing manager, animosities from existing marketing team members towards Teisha, misplaced alliances, and many other people problems Matt didn't identify or ignored before the change.

Understanding the difference between change and transition can help leaders plan appropriately. It is rare that change itself causes problems; typically, the culprit is a lack of transitional planning. Leaders are responsible for foreseeing and creating a strategy for transition in their organizations. But often, we spend so much time on change, we never strategically think through the transitional issues.

Understanding the difference between change and transition can help leaders plan appropriately.

TRANSITIONAL PLANS

To be a good CEO or pastor, it isn't enough to only think through what we're going to do. We must also take time to write down all of the contingencies and create a written transitional plan.

Before the change Matt should have made a list of all the issues he could foresee. What vacuum would he create with this change? In this case, the accounting department would be without a manager.

What situation results from this change? It appears that Teisha could be in a situation where her team doesn't respect her. As a leader, what can Matt do to help her earn the respect she needs? Can he pass some of his credibility on to her? Credibility is a people problem, but it's not the only relational problem to consider during a transition. Other personnel issues that need thought include:

- Which people does the change affect?

- Of those people, who are the ones who care?

- Who cares deeply?

- Of those who care deeply, who will be positive about this change and who will not?

The main question is: How do I position Teisha for success?

After thinking through these questions, the leader must create a written plan and then make strategic decisions based on the plan. For example, consider:

- How will I approach each person?

- How will I communicate the details to him or her?

- What information will that person need to understand this change?

Here's another illustration. Tim is our worship leader. He gets caught in some kind of sin, and we have to discipline him. We ask him to step down from his position. But problems arise when some of the women think we weren't hard enough on him, the men think we were too hard on him, the young people think there was nothing wrong with what he did, and the old people wonder how many leaders are also doing what Tim did. Tim's mama is upset; and his daddy, who is on the church board, is mad at the leadership.

See what is happening?

Moving him out of his role as worship leader was the change. It was not a big deal to make that change. What will come back to bite us are the transitional issues. We need to map out all the contingencies, knowing that some of these plans will happen and others we won't have to worry about. We can't plan everything, but as much as possible we want to think through the transitional issues.

Matt needs to think systemically about the change he's made. He needs to remember that a change in one department will affect all the other departments. It is systemic thinking. Once the transition is worked through and people feel secure, the change is a nonissue. Leading change is easy if we first understand how to manage the transition.

HOW TO TRANSITION

William Bridges is a noted expert on change and transition. In his most recent book, *Managing Transitions: Making the Most of Change,* he explains that the reason change agents fail is because they focus on the solution instead of the problem.

> **90 percent of a leader's efforts should be spent on selling the problem**

He believes that 90 percent of a leader's efforts should be spent on selling the problem and helping people understand what is *not* working. He rightly claims that people don't perceive the need for a solution if they don't have a problem.

Let's say I have an administrative assistant who is not working out. She comes in late, has a bad attitude, and is incompetent in her job. Firing her would solve that problem; but before I can fire her, I need to consider how this action would affect her coworkers. Currently she gets a lot of sympathy from them. They enable her behavior and encourage me to do the same by saying things like, "Don't you realize she's pregnant and recently had to change apartments?"

This is also where lawsuits can become transitional issues. Firing a pregnant woman without cause could bring legal trouble for me and the company. I must be sure the problem is understood. Of course, I am aware that she is failing to be a good assistant but I have to help others in the office understand that her inability to do her job is a problem for all of us. If I don't, they will be the first to undermine me by saying to the new assistant, "Did you know that he fired the pregnant woman who was here before you?"

So part of the transition must be helping people understand the problem, so they can more quickly agree on a solution.

In my book, *Who Moved Your Ladder?: Your Next Bold Move,* I spent a lot of time talking about transitional issues. I used the example of my resignation from Beulah Heights Bible College. Instead of just resigning, I personally traveled all over the country to meet with board members and tell them what I was going to do and why. I even developed a possible successor.

In making that change, I had a transition plan. I knew who I was going to talk to, when I was going to talk to them, and what I was going to say. I can vouch from my personal experience that the time spent thinking and planning the transition made what could have been a negative occurrence a time of positive growth for me and the college.

LEADERS ARE RESPONSIBLE FOR TRANSITIONS

A successful transition isn't the responsibility of the people undergoing the change. The responsibility for a successful transition belongs to the leader making the change. In one of my seminars, a young woman named Regina said she was moved from a small role in the children's department to a larger responsibility as Christian education minister. Regina did everything she could to prepare her people for a change. She found and trained her successor and helped transition her old team to their new leader.

But no one did the same for Regina. The pastor failed to make an announcement to the church that Regina was given this new responsibility. Further complicating matters, the former Christian education minister didn't realize that he was now out of a job and continued to function as if nothing had changed. This is a great example of a change without a transition. Regina had made the change; but without her pastor helping with the transition, she was now impotent in her new responsibility.

Some might wonder why a pastor would do that. I think I know. Regina is his daughter, and he was worried about how people would react to her taking on such an important role. He felt that she was the best person for the job, and she felt that she was ready. But without handling the transition properly, no one else at the church had that same confidence. Now he is trying to sort through the mess. He has both personal issues—after all, she's his daughter—and professional issues—his vision for this position in the church. In addition, when I first heard about the situation, Regina had been in her job for three months!

My recommendation to Regina was that her father go before the people and say, "My daughter, Regina, is going to provide great leadership to the Christian education ministry department at our church. Actually, she should have been functioning in this position for the last three months, but I have been remiss in not making that announcement. But I'm correcting that today. Come on up here, Regina, and tell them about your vision. What's God going to go with you?"

He will need to support her vision and have the people pray for her in her new role, sort of as a miniinauguration. But he has to say something like, "I was remiss in not doing this before," so the people will know why he is doing this now and not then.

Assimilating new people into leadership roles is the hardest change issue we face. However, if we as leaders are aware of the differences between transitions and changes, if we properly prepare and execute a transitional

> **Assimilating new people into leadership roles is the hardest change issue we face.**

plan, and if we take responsibility for the changes we bring on our people, the results will be worth the effort.

REVIEW & REFLECT

1. Change is the result of a decision.

2. Transition is the emotional, relational, financial, and psychological processing of change.

3. Change is external. Transitions are internal.

4. Change can often be smooth. Transitions rarely are.

5. Leaders are responsible for foreseeing and creating a strategy for transition in their organizations.

6. A transitional plan must take into account all the contingencies, and it must be written down.

7. Leaders should consider the following two questions: What vacuum will be created with this change? What situation is created as a result of this change?

8. Other personnel issues that should be considered are:

    - Which people will be affected by the change?

    - Of those people, who are the ones who care?

    - Who cares deeply?

    - Of those who care deeply, who will be positive about this change? Who will be negative?

9. The transitional plan should include actions that need to be taken for each person involved and include instruction on:

    - How will I approach this person?

    - How will I communicate the details to him or her?

    - What information will this person need to understand this change?

10. William Bridges, the change expert, believes 90 percent of a leader's efforts should be spent on selling the problem. People don't need a solution if they don't have a problem.

11. A successful transition isn't the responsibility of the people undergoing the change. The responsibility for a successful transition belongs to the leader making the change.

12. Assimilating new people into leadership roles is the hardest change and transition issue we face.

7

TEACHING POINTS & DISCUSSION GUIDE

INTRODUCTION

Teaching Points

- Change isn't inherently bad or good... it's how we prepare for and respond to change that makes it work for or against us.

- Change brings turbulence into organizations.

- By far, leaders influence the quality of the experience people have more than any turbulent organizational changes do.

- During the storms of change, people expect more from leaders than they do during stable times.

- Storms bring out the leader within you.

- The best thing leaders can do to weather the storm of change is to prepare for it.

- The two greatest factors to outlasting and thriving through any storm are preparation and leadership.

Discussion Questions

1. In what ways are you prepared for change? In what ways could you be better prepared?

2. The authors assert, "The worst thing that you could do as a pilot in a storm is flying as if there weren't one". Are there any storms you are flying through yet ignoring? If you fast-forward this movie, how would it play out if you do nothing?

3. Within every storm lie opportunities. What opportunities could open for you on the other side of change?

4. What would it look like for your entire crew (team) to be on the same page?

CHAPTER 1
WEATHERING THE STORM:
LEADING IN UNCERTAIN TIMES

Teaching Points

- Vision is the where.

- Strategy is the how.

- Your strategy may change; your vision doesn't.

- You may need to change your route but not your vision.

- Vision keeps you headed in the right direction despite unforeseen obstacles.

- Vision always proceeds planning. Before you plan a change or lead through uncertainty you must start with your vision.

- The winds of change have increased the likelihood of an organizational disaster.

- A disaster is anything that significantly affects your ability to carry out the critical functions and mission of your organization.

- Preparation (plans, systems) and leadership (insightful, courageous, and innovative top-tier leaders) are the biggest factors for outlasting any storm.

Discussion Questions

1. Describe how your vision would look once you arrived there.

2. In what ways, if any, have you been sidetracked from your vision?

3. What's taken a visionary "back seat" that needs to be moved back to the forefront again?

4. What are your organizational critical functions? What is your back-up plan should one of them be threatened? For help creating a disaster recovery plan visit www. InfluencersGlobal.com/myplan.

5. As a leader(s) what is your next courageous move?

6. What would it look like for your organization to move forward in innovative ways?

CHAPTER 2
FIREFIGHTERS:
POSITIONED TO PROTECT

Teaching Points

- Most fires can be prevented or at least minimized.

- People who are inside your house will start nearly all fires you face.

- Often it's the "who" that show up first to a fire that extinguishes or escalates its damage.

- Organizational fires always involve people and how leadership responds always determines the damage done.

- Firefighters should be your first responders to organizational fires.

- Firefighters are leaders that are identified, equipped and empowered protectors of your vision and purpose.

- Firefighters model organizational values, silently teach people how to behave in ways that are consistent with what the organization represents, and remind others why "we" always do certain things and why "we" never do other things.

- There aren't any fireproof organizations but you can create a flame-resistant culture where conflict isn't the norm but the exception.

- Words create culture.

- Words cause more fires than anything else.

- Backburner issues must be watched. They are smoldering and can quickly start a fire.

- You can put out some fires internally; other fires require outside help to extinguish.

Discussion Questions

1. Who are your firefighters and what do they need from you to best protect your vision?

2. What organizational values do your firefighters model? Specifically, what behaviors do they silently model for others to follow?

3. What could you do to better the quality of firefighters positioned to protect your vision? What could you do to multiply the quantity of firefighters to protect your vision?

4. Historically what type of words escalated fires in your context? What words extinguished them? What can you learn from this and apply to the future?

CHAPTER 3
EARTHQUAKES: WHEN VALUES COLLIDE

Teaching Points

- Values drive human behavior.

- Your values, consciously and subconsciously, influence your thoughts, feelings, and actions

- When people within the same organization don't have shared values the organization suffers from regular tremors and haphazard quakes.

- Organizational values are the few non-negotiable and enduring virtues that your organization is built on. They fuel vision, simplify choices, unify efforts and clarify behavior.

- No matter what you do, you will always lose people; however, when you have shared values you decide which ones you keep.

- A lack of shared values results in a misaligned organization and can lead to an organizational split.

- Whenever an organization is out of alignment it creates an atmosphere for storms.

- Whenever things are perfectly aligned new doors of opportunity open.

Discussion Questions

1. What does your organization value? How do you know?

2. What would a first-timer or an outsider say your organization values? Does this differ from what you say it values? If so, how? What do you attribute the difference to? Explain.

3. Think about your last "earthquake". Can you identify the differences between what one person/group valued as opposed to the other?

4. Imagine if all stakeholders shared the same organizational values. How could things have turned out differently?

5. Do you think you can get to your vision without shared values? Explain.

6. What doors of opportunity could open if things in your organization were perfectly aligned?

CHAPTER 4
THE LEADER AND HIS RELATIONSHIPS

Teaching Points

- As a leader, your future and all those with you depend on both those you retain and those you release.

- Toxic relationships are relationships that are life taking not life giving.

- Leaders must keenly manage both the places and spaces that people have in their lives.

- The place a person has involves their role, the space they fill considers the level of intimacy shared.

- No matter how seemingly successful a leader appears in public, it is his or her private life that ultimately determines public success.

- All leaders need people around them who challenge and sharpen them.

- A leader's greatest ability is responsibility.

- Leadership always involves other people.

- Every relationship is either increasing in value or decreasing in value depending on how much you invest in it.

- Ladder holders are strong, attentive, faithful, firm and loyal.

- The voices in your ear will determine your life's direction.

Discussion Questions

1. When two people walk together one person always sets the pace. Who have you allowed to set your pace? Whose pace are you setting?

2. Who has clear discernment to help you better manage the people who occupy specific places and spaces in your life? Specifically how can they help you?

3. In general, management involves things but leadership always involves people. What systems can you put in place to better manage things so you can focus more on leading people?

4. As a leader, what is your greatest weakness? How can you strengthen that area?

5. As a leader what is your greatest strength? How can you build on it?

6. Who's holding your ladder? What could they do to help you climb higher?

7. Whose ladder are you holding? What do they need from you to climb higher?

CHAPTER 5
DISASTER RECOVERY: MISSION STILL POSSIBLE

Teaching Points

- You can recover from virtually any storm, you've prepared for, with resiliency and adaptability.

- Rapid and constant changes require resiliency and adaptability.

- Resiliency is the ability to recover quickly from setbacks.

- Storms cause setbacks.

- All setbacks cost something (time, resources, opportunity, etc.).

- Adaptability is the ability to change easily.

- Despite ongoing changes, you should still plan; just in pencil.

- Changing conditions require you to rethink how you do what you do.

- Many disasters could totally be avoided with planning.

- Other disasters could be overcome when leaders and their teams are resilient and adaptable.

- Disasters can be defining moments.

- Disasters don't have to be repeated. They can be isolated incidents and not necessarily the rule.

- Don't make long-term decisions based on disastrous events.

- Use disasters to learn from them.

- Be flexible. Disaster recovery is harder for those who cannot bend when the situation requires doing so.

Discussion Questions

1. In what ways have you had to be resilient in the past? What can you learn from then that could help you now and in the future?

2. How can you build adaptability into the DNA of your team?

3. What do you and your team do that may require rethinking how you do what you do?

4. What disasters are you most prepared for? Which are you least prepared for?

5. If you began preparing for disasters from the least to the greatest, which one disaster would take the least amount of effort to prepare for?

6. Looking back to previous disasters what lessons can you gleam from then to help you better prepare for tomorrow?

CHAPTER 6
FINDING COURAGE FACING CHANGE

Teaching Points

- Leaders don't lose people when they're traveling straight. They lose them in the transitions when they make a turn.

- Change happens in a moment. Transition happens over time.

- All leaders, not just senior leaders, are responsible for leading transition within the organization.

- Leaders are departmental and organizational GPS' that announce a change or a "turn" is coming, giving people ample time to effectively transition.

- Leaders should spend the vast majority of their efforts on transitions not changes.

- People can't get beyond what they haven't gotten over. In order to lead people forward, you may need to go backwards to meet them where they really are not where you thought they should be now.

- People accept change within an adapter group: innovators, early adopters, early majority, late majority and laggards.

- The innovators and adopters will "get it" quick and the laggards may never "get it". Focus the majority of your efforts on the early majority and late majority.

- Change is inevitable; growth is optional.

- Change is the result of a decision.

- Transition is the emotional, relational, financial, and psychological processing of change.

- Change is external. Transitions are internal.

- Change can often be smooth. Transitions rarely are.

- Leaders are responsible for foreseeing and creating a strategy for transition in their organizations.

- A transitional plan must take into account all the contingencies, and it must be written down.

- The transitional plan should include actions that need to be taken for each person involved and include instruction on: How will I approach this person? How will I communicate the details to him or her? What information will this person need to understand this change? For coaching on creating a transitional and communication plan visit www.InfluencersGlobal.com/ myplan.

- William Bridges, the change expert, believes 90 percent of a leader's efforts should be spent on selling the problem. People don't need a solution if they don't have a problem.

- A successful transition isn't the responsibility of the people undergoing the change. The responsibility for a successful transition belongs to the leader making the change.

- Assimilating new people into leadership roles is the hardest change and transition issue we face.

Discussion Questions

1. What was the last change you made or were a part of? How well did people affected by the change transition?

2. Who's stuck in the last change? What do they need from you or other leaders to move forward? (Support, empathy, information, time, clarity, etc.)

3. What future change(s) are you or your leaders considering? What vacuum will be created with this change? What situation may be created as a result of this change?

4. Other personnel issues that should be considered before a change are: Which people will be affected by the change? Of those people, who are the ones who care? Who cares deeply? Of those who care deeply, who will be positive about this change? Who will be negative?

APPENDIX

The Well Curve

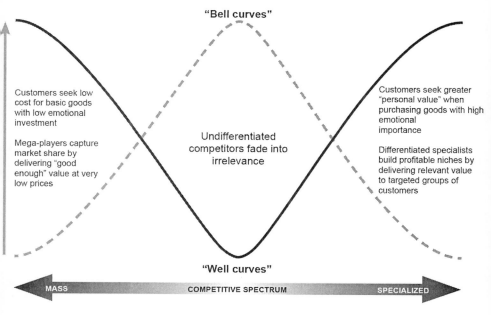

"Bell curves"

Customers seek low cost for basic goods with low emotional investment

Mega-players capture market share by delivering "good enough" value at very low prices

Undifferentiated competitors fade into irrelevance

Customers seek greater "personal value" when purchasing goods with high emotional importance

Differentiated specialists build profitable niches by delivering relevant value to targeted groups of customers

"Well curves"

MASS ◄───── COMPETITIVE SPECTRUM ─────► SPECIALIZED

Source: IBM Institute for Business Value. The "well curve" concept was described in the following article: Pink, Daniel H. "The Shape of Things to Come." Wired. May 2003.

ABOUT
DR. DON BRAWLEY III

Dr. Don Brawley III is a *Leadership Strategist* who helps influencers reach their dreams faster. He is the founder and CEO of Influencers Global, a company committed to helping leaders increase their influence, income, and impact for God's Kingdom. He along with his wife Mona are the founding pastors of Canaan Land Church International a thriving ministry in suburban Atlanta, Georgia.

Dr. Don earned his Masters of Organizational Leadership (2004) and Doctorate in Strategic Leadership, with a coaching emphasis (2008), from Regent University's School of Global Leadership and Entrepreneurship.

Dr. Don travels nationally and abroad consulting and coaching pastors, marketplace and non-profit leaders, facilitating leadership roundtables, and delivering motivational, practical and inspiring messages. He's a highly sought after consultant, coach, and conference speaker. He's trained leaders for Fortune 500 companies such as UPS and educational institutions such as The University of Phoenix.

Additionally, Dr. Brawley has published several works. Most recently, he co-authored, *Weathering the Storm: Leading in Uncertain Times Deluxe Edition* with Dr. Samuel R. Chand. The original release has become a favorite on four continents and has recently been translated to Portuguese.

In March 2015, he was honored, with a resolution, by the Georgia House of Representatives for his leadership accomplishments. Later in 2015, Dr. Don made history when he held the first ever global online conference in the Kingdom spanning 6 days across 3 continents.

Don has been married to his high school sweetheart Mona for nearly 30 years. Together they are the proud parents of three children: Brandon (Kristie), Chantelle, and Aaron.

For more information concerning Don Brawley you may visit www.canaanlandchurch.org | www.influencersglobal.com

ABOUT
DR. SAMUEL R. CHAND

Who would have thought, when in 1973 *"student"* Samuel Chand was serving Beulah Heights Bible College as janitor, cook and dishwasher, that he would return in 1989 as *"President"* of the same college! Under his leadership it became the country's largest predominantly African-American Bible College.

Dr. Chand is a former Pastor, college President, Chancellor and now serves as President Emeritus of Beulah Heights University.

In this season of his life, Dr. Chand does *one* thing--Leadership. His singular vision for his life is to **Help Others Succeed.**

Dr. Chand develops leaders through:

- Leadership Consultations

- Leadership Resources—Books, CDs, DVDs

- Leadership Speaking

- Dream Releaser Coaching

- Dream Releaser Publishing

As a **Dream Releaser** he serves Pastors, ministries and businesses as a *Leadership Architect* and *Change Strategist*. Dr. Chand speaks regularly at leadership conferences, churches, corporations, ministerial conferences, seminars and other leadership development opportunities.

Dr. Chand...

- Consults with large churches and businesses on leadership and capacity enhancing issues

- Named in the top-30 global *Leadership Gurus* list

- Founder & President of Dream Releaser Coaching and Dream Releaser Publishing

- Conducts international Leadership Conferences

- Serves on the board of Beulah Heights University

- Serves on the board of Advisors of EQUIP (Dr. John Maxwell's ministry), equipping 5 million leaders world-wide

- Serves as National Board Member for Calcutta Mercy Ministries

Dr. Chand has authored and published 14 books:

FAILURE: *The Womb of Success*

FUTURING: *Leading your Church into Tomorrow*

WHO'S HOLDING YOUR LADDER?:
Selecting your Leaders--your most crucial decision

WHO MOVED YOUR LADDER?: *Your Next Bold Move*

WHAT'S SHAKIN' YOUR LADDER?:
15 Challenges All Leaders Face

LADDER*Shifts: New realities—Rapid change—Your destiny*

LADDER FOCUS:
Creating, Sustaining, and Enlarging Your BIG Picture

PLANNING YOUR SUCCESSION:
Preparing for Your Future

REChurch: *When Change is no Longer an Option*

MASTER LEADERS—*A collaborative book
with George Barna*

WEATHERING THE STORM:
Leading in Uncertain Times

CRACKING YOUR CHURCH'S CULTURE CODE:
Seven Keys to Unleashing Vision & Inspiration

LEADERSHIP PAIN: *The Classroom For Growth*
BIGGER FASTER LEADERSHIP:
Lessons From The Builders of the Panama Canal

Leaders are using Dr. Chand's books as handbooks worldwide in leadership development.

His educational background includes two honorary degrees. A Doctor of Humane Letters from Beulah Heights University and a Doctor of Divinity from Heritage Bible College, a Master of Arts in Biblical Counseling from Grace Theological Seminary, and a Bachelor of Arts in Biblical Education from Beulah Heights University.

Dr. Chand shares his life and love with his wife Brenda, two daughters Rachel & Deborah, son-in-law Zack and granddaughters Adeline and Rose.

Being raised in a Pastor's home in India has uniquely equipped Dr. Chand to share his passion--that of mentoring, developing and inspiring leaders to break all limits—in ministry and the marketplace.